TRADING
SUCCESS LOGBOOK

TRACK TRADES • MASTER STRATEGIES
GROW PROFITS

BengalGeek

Explore other publications:

Scan me!

This logbook Belongs To:

INTRODUCTION & HOW TO USE THIS LOGBOOK

Welcome to Your Trading Success Journey

This logbook is designed to help you trade with clarity, discipline, and confidence. Whether you're a beginner or experienced trader, writing down your trades and reflecting on your process will sharpen your skills and boost your consistency.

WHY KEEP A TRADING LOG?

- It reveals patterns in your winning and losing trades.
- It reduces emotional decision-making by creating structure.
- It helps you track strategies, refine risk management, and avoid repeated mistakes.

MY TOP 3 GOALS FOR THIS LOGBOOK:

1. ______________________________
2. ______________________________
3. ______________________________

MY TRADING PLAN

Define Your Personal Trading Blueprint

Successful traders don't rely on luck– they follow a clear, consistent plan. Use this page to set your rules and stick to them.

My Trading Style (check all that apply):

☐ Scalping
☐ Day Trading
☐ Swing Trading
☐ Position Trading

My Preferred Currency Pairs:

____

My Maximum Daily Loss Limit:

$ ______________________________

My Profit Target Per Week:

$ ______________________________

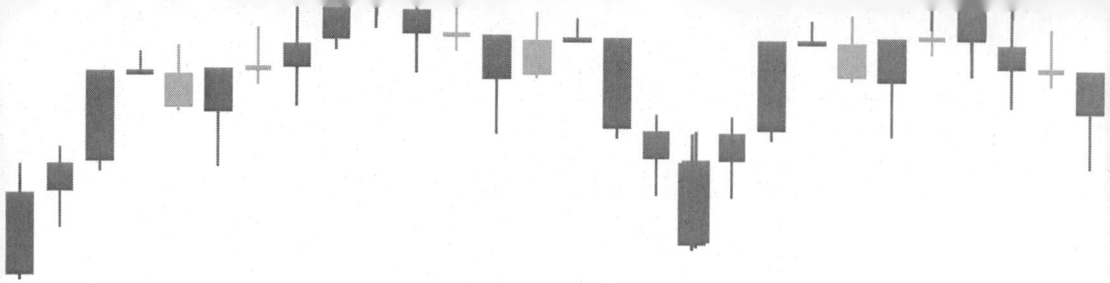

TRADING EMOTIONS

SCARED TIRED SAD HAPPY EXCITED

Notes

DAILY TRADING LOG

Date	Time	Currency Pair	Buy/Sell	Entry Price	Closing	Trade Size

Reason for Entry	Strategy Used	Trade Size
(pattern, news, signal):		

Reason for Entry (pattern, news, signal):

Strategy Used:

Emotional State When Entering Trade:

What I Learned:

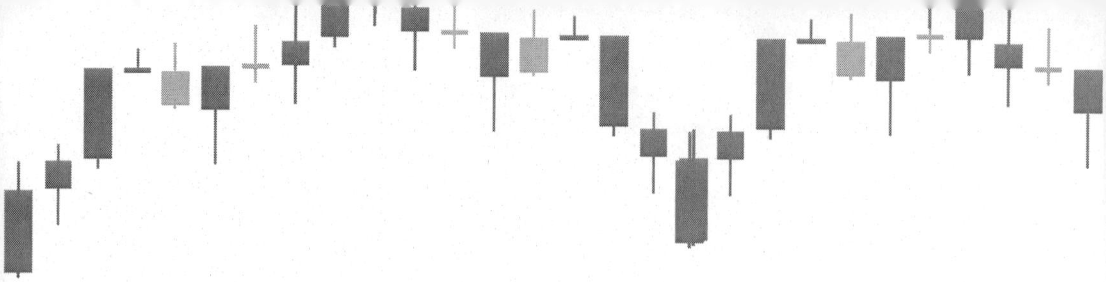

Notes

DAILY TRADING LOG

Date	Time	Currency Pair	Buy/Sell	Entry Price	Closing	Trade Size

Reason for Entry	Strategy Used	Trade Size
(pattern, news, signal):		

Reason for Entry (pattern, news, signal):

Strategy Used:

Emotional State When Entering Trade:

What I Learned:

Notes

DAILY TRADING LOG

Date	Time	Currency Pair	Buy/Sell	Entry Price	Closing	Trade Size

Reason for Entry	Strategy Used	Trade Size
(pattern, news, signal):		

Reason for Entry (pattern, news, signal):

Strategy Used:

Emotional State When Entering Trade:

What I Learned:

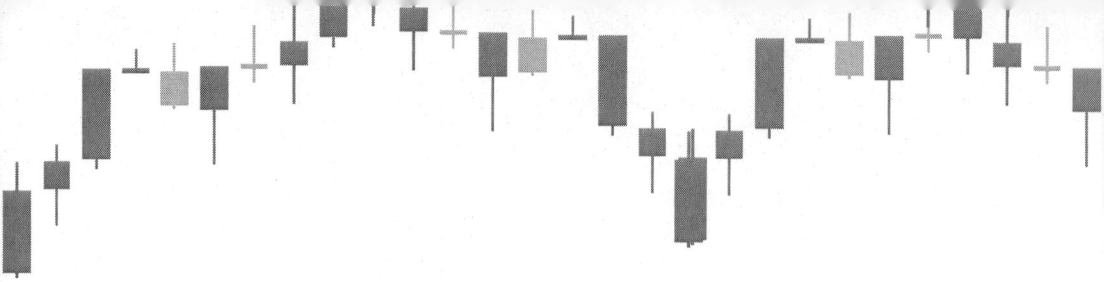

Notes

DAILY TRADING LOG

Date	Time	Currency Pair	Buy/Sell	Entry Price	Closing	Trade Size

Reason for Entry	Strategy Used	Trade Size
(pattern, news, signal):		

Reason for Entry (pattern, news, signal):

Strategy Used:

Emotional State When Entering Trade:

What I Learned:

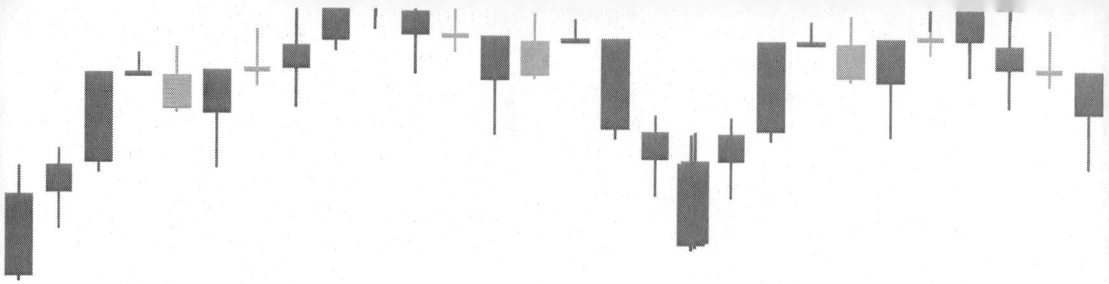

Notes

DAILY TRADING LOG

Date	Time	Currency Pair	Buy/Sell	Entry Price	Closing	Trade Size

Reason for Entry	Strategy Used	Trade Size
(pattern, news, signal):		

Reason for Entry (pattern, news, signal):

Strategy Used:

Emotional State When Entering Trade:

What I Learned:

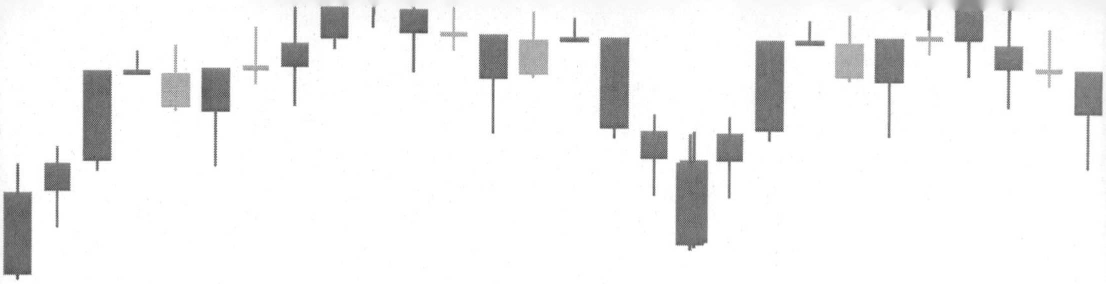

Notes

Weekly Review & Reflection

Weekly Overview

Total Trades Taken: _____ Wins: ___________

Win/Loss Ratio: _________ Win/Loss Prólc

My Biggest Win This Week:

____

____

____

My Biggest Loss This Week:

____

____

Top 3 Lessons Learned:

1. ____
2. ____
3. ____

One Improvement I'll Make Next Week:

____

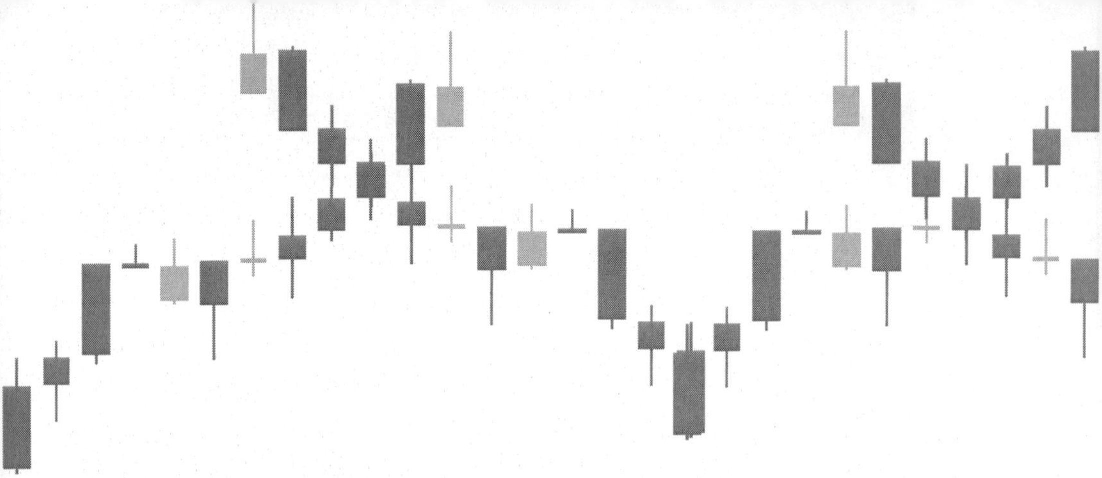

Notes

MY TRADING PLAN

Define Your Personal Trading Blueprint

Successful traders don't rely on luck– they follow a clear, consistent plan. Use this page to set your rules and stick to them.

My Trading Style (check all that apply):

- ☐ Scalping
- ☐ Day Trading
- ☐ Swing Trading
- ☐ Position Trading

My Preferred Currency Pairs:

____

My Maximum Daily Loss Limit:

$ ______________________________________

My Profit Target Per Week:

$ ______________________________________

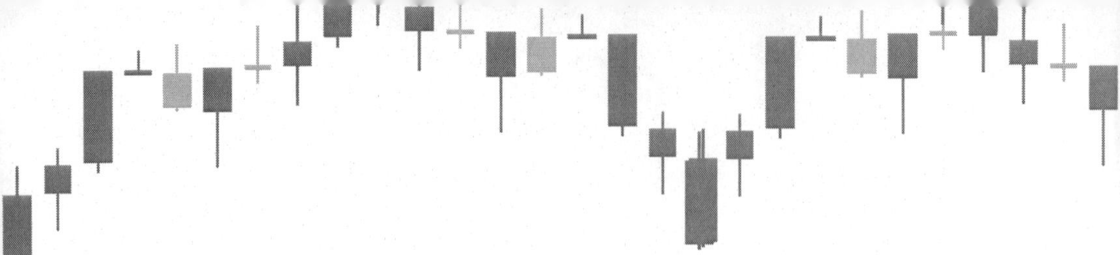

TRADING EMOTIONS

SCARED TIRED SAD HAPPY EXCITED

Notes

DAILY TRADING LOG

Date	Time	Currency Pair	Buy/Sell	Entry Price	Closing	Trade Size

Reason for Entry	Strategy Used	Trade Size
(pattern, news, signal):		

Reason for Entry (pattern, news, signal):

Strategy Used:

Emotional State When Entering Trade:

What I Learned:

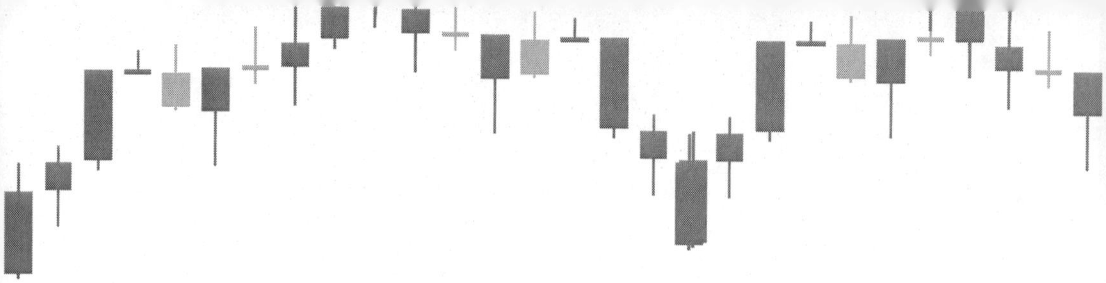

Notes

DAILY TRADING LOG

Date	Time	Currency Pair	Buy/Sell	Entry Price	Closing	Trade Size

Reason for Entry	Strategy Used	Trade Size
(pattern, news, signal):		

Reason for Entry (pattern, news, signal):

Strategy Used:

Emotional State When Entering Trade:

What I Learned:

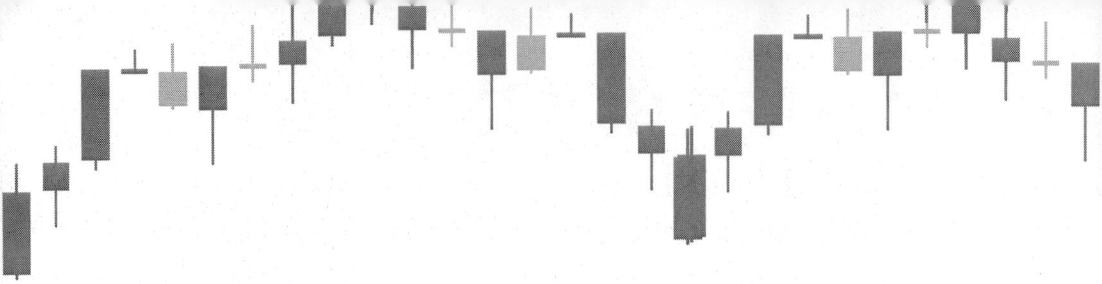

Notes

DAILY TRADING LOG

Date	Time	Currency Pair	Buy/Sell	Entry Price	Closing	Trade Size

Reason for Entry	Strategy Used	Trade Size
(pattern, news, signal):		

Reason for Entry (pattern, news, signal):

Strategy Used:

Emotional State When Entering Trade:

What I Learned:

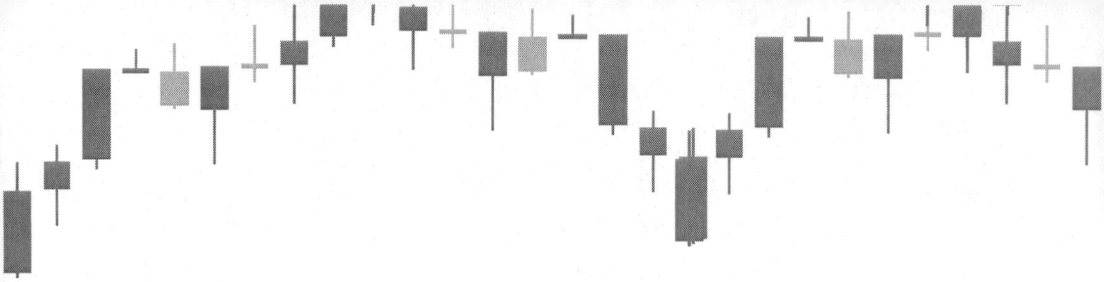

Notes

DAILY TRADING LOG

Date	Time	Currency Pair	Buy/Sell	Entry Price	Closing	Trade Size

Reason for Entry	Strategy Used	Trade Size
(pattern, news, signal):		

Reason for Entry (pattern, news, signal):

Strategy Used:

Emotional State When Entering Trade:

What I Learned:

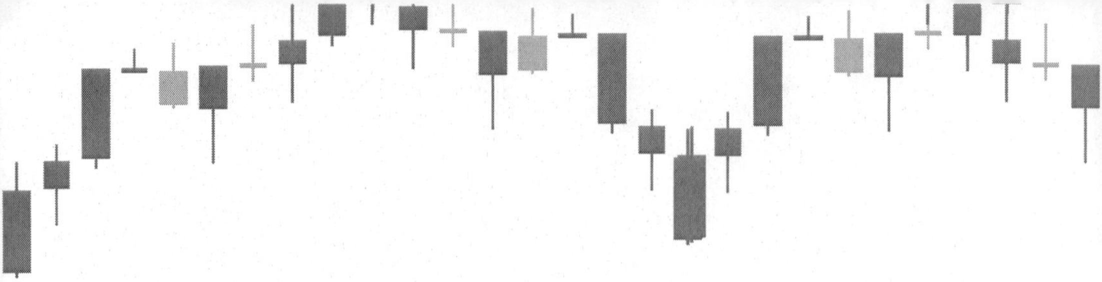

Notes

DAILY TRADING LOG

Date	Time	Currency Pair	Buy/Sell	Entry Price	Closing	Trade Size

Reason for Entry	Strategy Used	Trade Size
(pattern, news, signal):		

Reason for Entry (pattern, news, signal):

Strategy Used:

Emotional State When Entering Trade:

What I Learned:

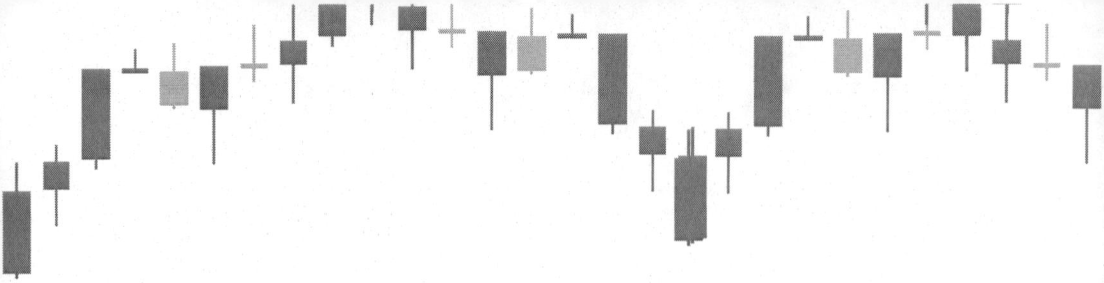

Notes

Weekly Review & Reflection

Weekly Overview

Total Trades Taken: _____ Wins: ___________

Win/Loss Ratio: _________ Win/Loss Prólc

My Biggest Win This Week:

____

____

____

My Biggest Loss This Week:

____

____

3 Top 3 Lessons Learned:

1. ____
2. ____
3. ____

One Improvement I'll Make Next Week:

____

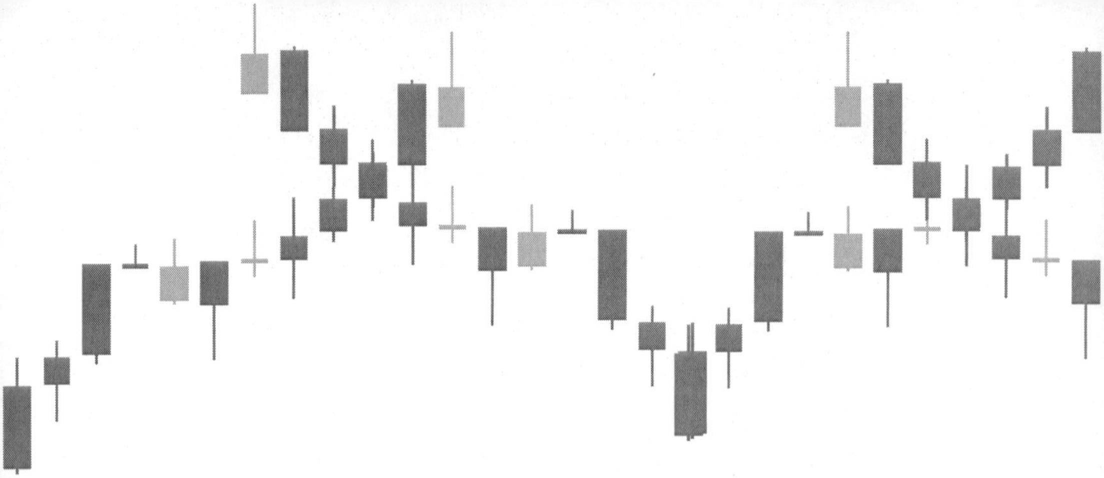

Notes

MY TRADING PLAN

Define Your Personal Trading Blueprint

Successful traders don't rely on luck– they follow a clear, consistent plan. Use this page to set your rules and stick to them.

My Trading Style (check all that apply):

- ☐ Scalping
- ☐ Day Trading
- ☐ Swing Trading
- ☐ Position Trading

My Preferred Currency Pairs:

____

My Maximum Daily Loss Limit:

$ ____________________________________

My Profit Target Per Week:

$ ____________________________________

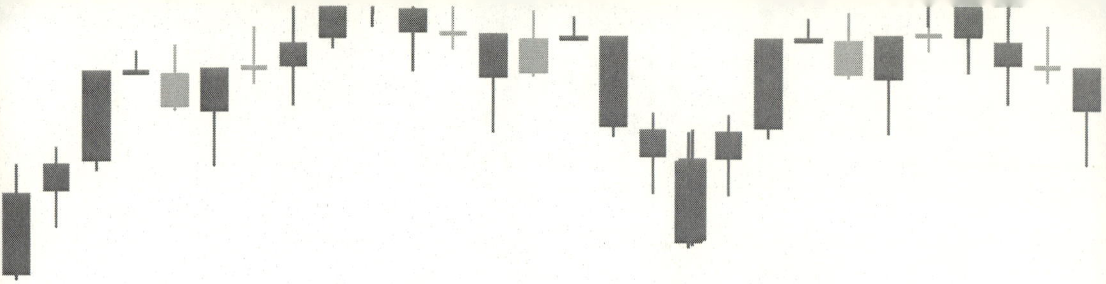

TRADING EMOTIONS

SCARED TIRED SAD HAPPY EXCITED

Notes

DAILY TRADING LOG

Date	Time	Currency Pair	Buy/Sell	Entry Price	Closing	Trade Size

Reason for Entry	Strategy Used	Trade Size
(pattern, news, signal):		

Reason for Entry (pattern, news, signal):

Strategy Used:

Emotional State When Entering Trade:

What I Learned:

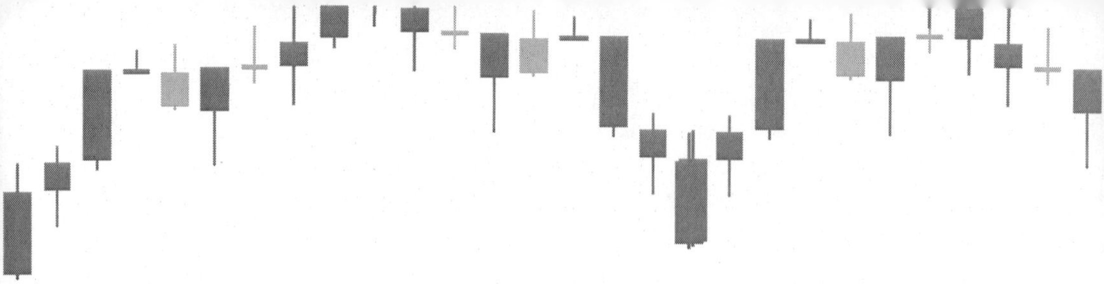

Notes

DAILY TRADING LOG

Date	Time	Currency Pair	Buy/Sell	Entry Price	Closing	Trade Size

Reason for Entry	Strategy Used	Trade Size
(pattern, news, signal):		

Reason for Entry (pattern, news, signal):

Strategy Used:

Emotional State When Entering Trade:

What I Learned:

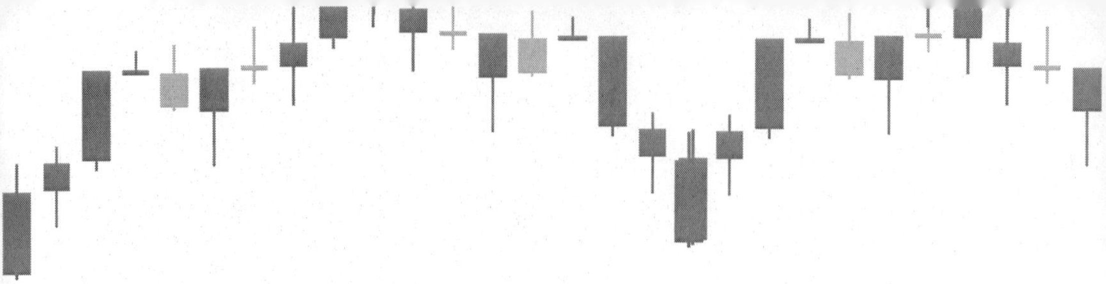

Notes

DAILY TRADING LOG

Date	Time	Currency Pair	Buy/Sell	Entry Price	Closing	Trade Size

Reason for Entry	Strategy Used	Trade Size
(pattern, news, signal):		

Reason for Entry (pattern, news, signal):

Strategy Used:

Emotional State When Entering Trade:

What I Learned:

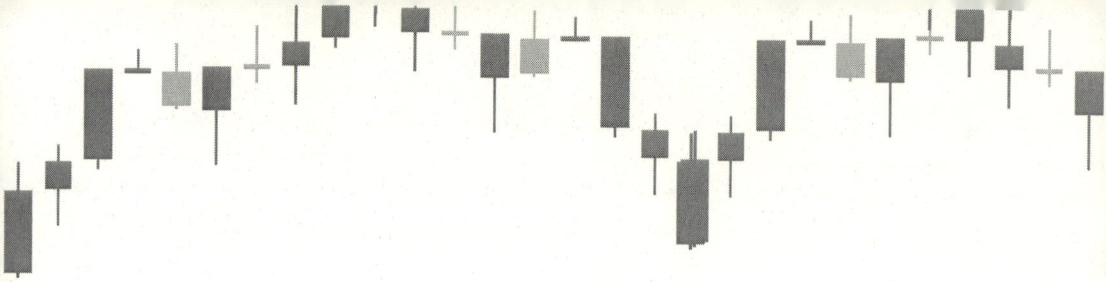

Notes

DAILY TRADING LOG

Date	Time	Currency Pair	Buy/Sell	Entry Price	Closing	Trade Size

Reason for Entry	Strategy Used	Trade Size
(pattern, news, signal):		

Reason for Entry (pattern, news, signal):

Strategy Used:

Emotional State When Entering Trade:

What I Learned:

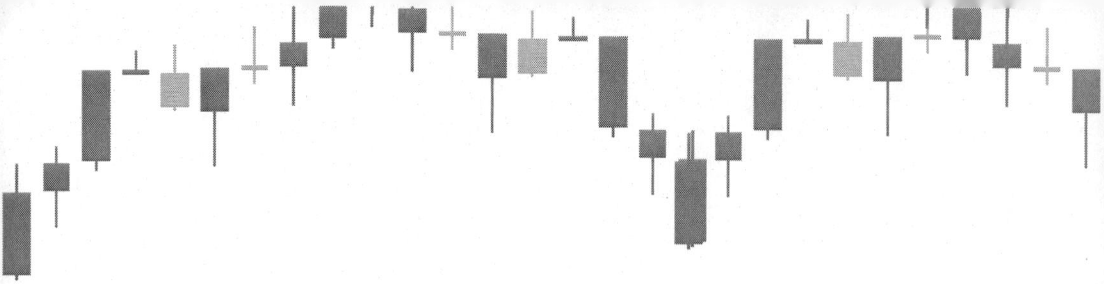

Notes

DAILY TRADING LOG

Date	Time	Currency Pair	Buy/Sell	Entry Price	Closing	Trade Size

Reason for Entry	Strategy Used	Trade Size
(pattern, news, signal):		

Reason for Entry (pattern, news, signal):

Strategy Used:

Emotional State When Entering Trade:

What I Learned:

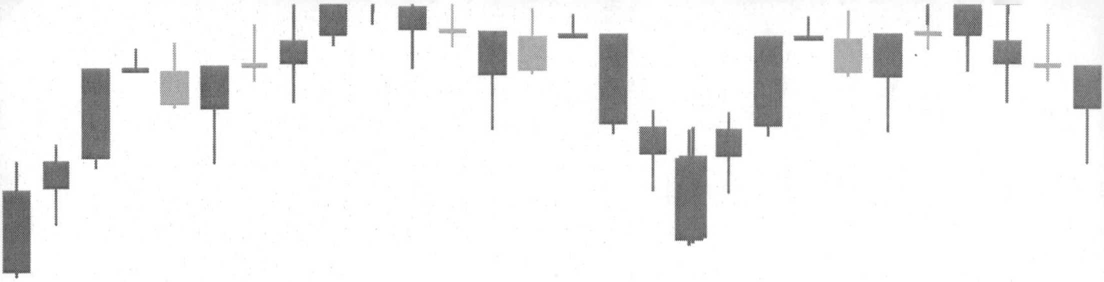

Notes

Weekly Review & Reflection

Weekly Overview

Total Trades Taken: _____ Wins: ___________

Win/Loss Ratio: _________ Win/Loss Prólc

My Biggest Win This Week:

____

____

____

My Biggest Loss This Week:

____

____

Top 3 Lessons Learned:

1. ____
2. ____
3. ____

One Improvement I'll Make Next Week:

____

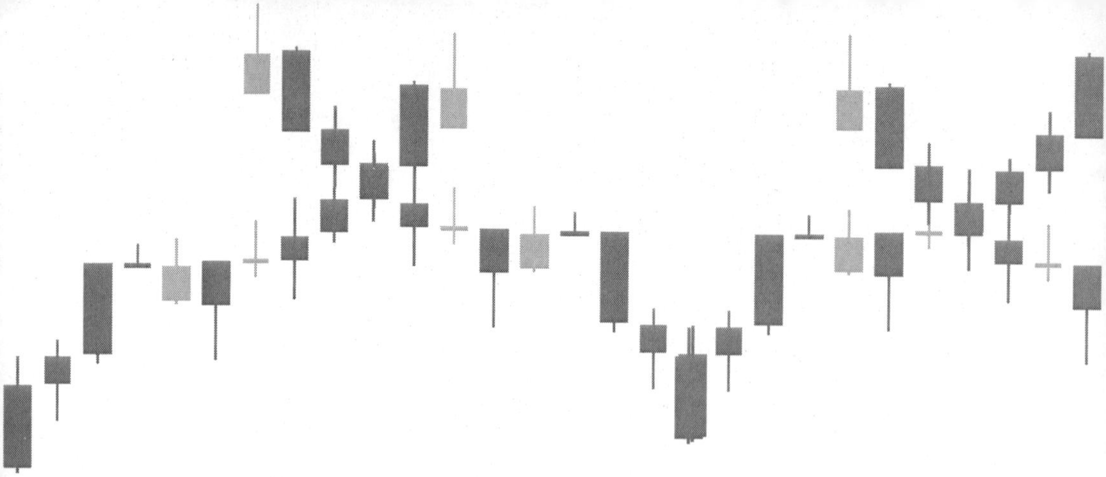

Notes

MY TRADING PLAN

Define Your Personal Trading Blueprint

Successful traders don't rely on luck– they follow a clear, consistent plan. Use this page to set your rules and stick to them.

My Trading Style (check all that apply):

- ☐ Scalping
- ☐ Day Trading
- ☐ Swing Trading
- ☐ Position Trading

My Preferred Currency Pairs:

____

My Maximum Daily Loss Limit:

$ ___________________________________

My Profit Target Per Week:

$ ___________________________________

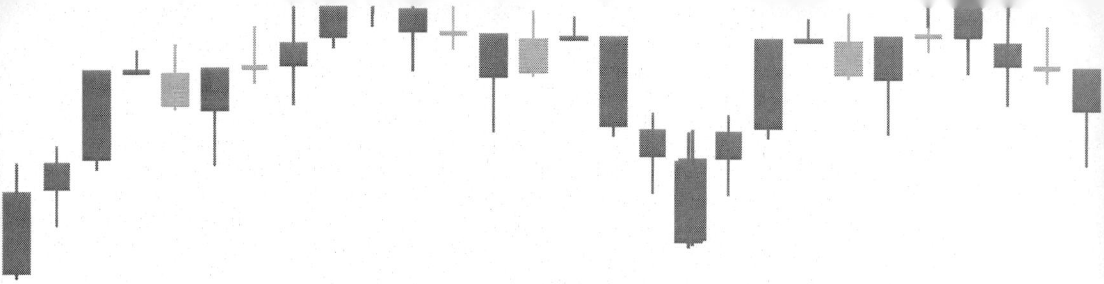

TRADING EMOTIONS

SCARED TIRED SAD HAPPY EXCITED

Notes

DAILY TRADING LOG

Date	Time	Currency Pair	Buy/Sell	Entry Price	Closing	Trade Size

Reason for Entry	Strategy Used	Trade Size
(pattern, news, signal):		

Reason for Entry (pattern, news, signal):

Strategy Used:

Emotional State When Entering Trade:

What I Learned:

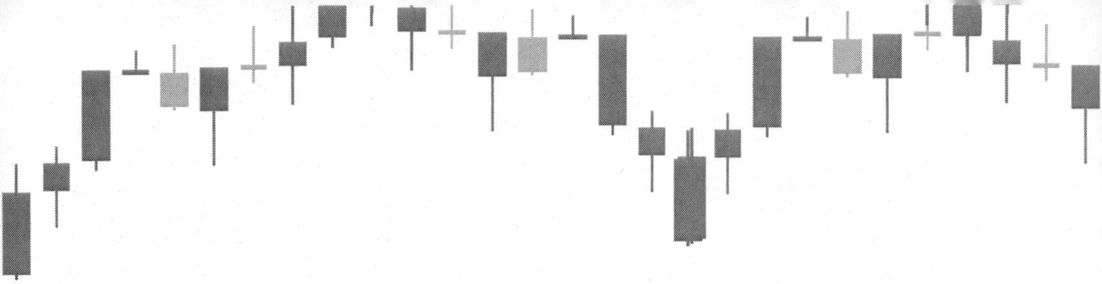

Notes

DAILY TRADING LOG

Date	Time	Currency Pair	Buy/Sell	Entry Price	Closing	Trade Size

Reason for Entry	Strategy Used	Trade Size
(pattern, news, signal):		

Reason for Entry (pattern, news, signal):

Strategy Used:

Emotional State When Entering Trade:

What I Learned:

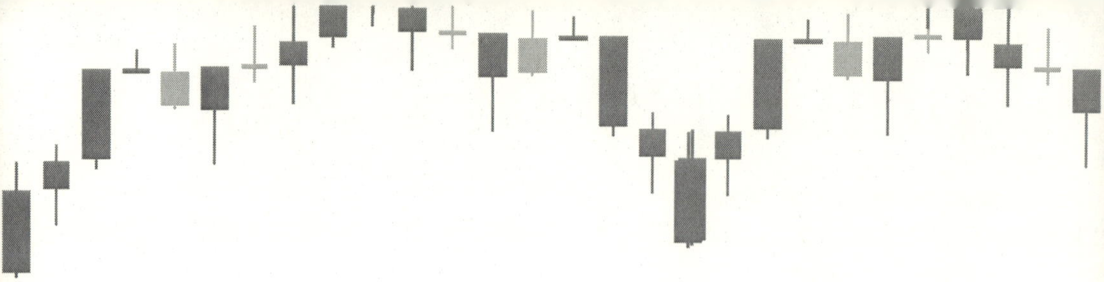

Notes

DAILY TRADING LOG

Date	Time	Currency Pair	Buy/Sell	Entry Price	Closing	Trade Size

Reason for Entry	Strategy Used	Trade Size
(pattern, news, signal):		

Reason for Entry (pattern, news, signal):

Strategy Used:

Emotional State When Entering Trade:

What I Learned:

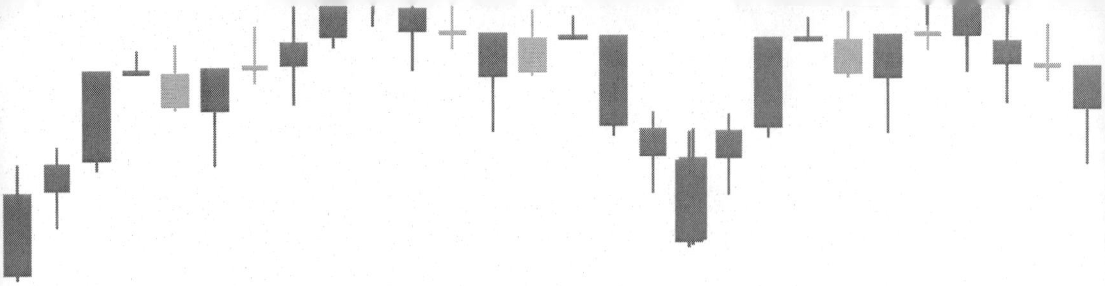

Notes

DAILY TRADING LOG

Date	Time	Currency Pair	Buy/Sell	Entry Price	Closing	Trade Size

Reason for Entry	Strategy Used	Trade Size
(pattern, news, signal):		

Reason for Entry (pattern, news, signal):

Strategy Used:

Emotional State When Entering Trade:

What I Learned:

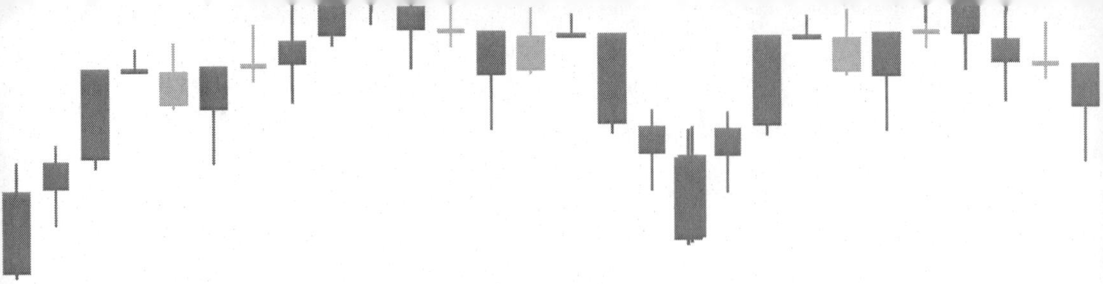

Notes

DAILY TRADING LOG

Date	Time	Currency Pair	Buy/Sell	Entry Price	Closing	Trade Size

Reason for Entry	Strategy Used	Trade Size
(pattern, news, signal):		

Reason for Entry (pattern, news, signal):

Strategy Used:

Emotional State When Entering Trade:

What I Learned:

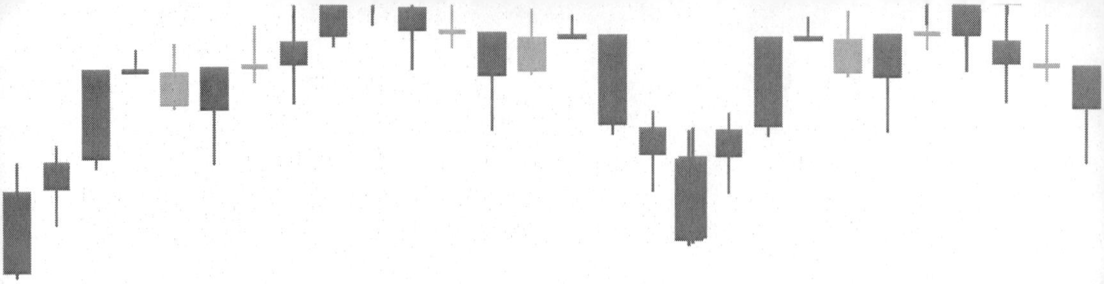

Notes

Weekly Review & Reflection

Weekly Overview

Total Trades Taken: _____ Wins: ___________

Win/Loss Ratio: _________ Win/Loss Prólc

My Biggest Win This Week:

____

____

____

My Biggest Loss This Week:

____

____

3 Top 3 Lessons Learned:

1. ____
2. ____
3. ____

One Improvement I'll Make Next Week:

____

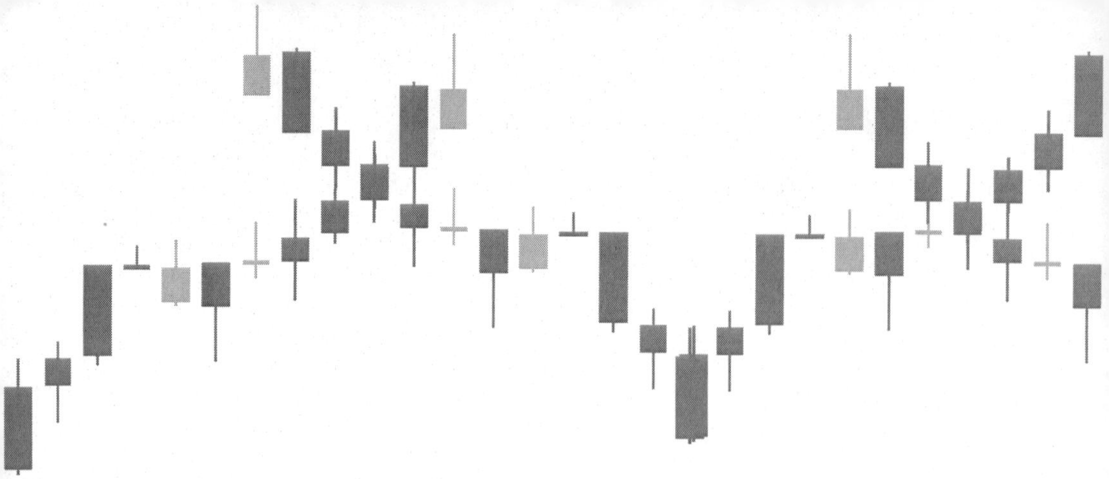

Notes

MY TRADING PLAN

Define Your Personal Trading Blueprint

Successful traders don't rely on luck– they follow a clear, consistent plan. Use this page to set your rules and stick to them.

My Trading Style (check all that apply):

- ☐ Scalping
- ☐ Day Trading
- ☐ Swing Trading
- ☐ Position Trading

My Preferred Currency Pairs:

____

My Maximum Daily Loss Limit:

$ ____

My Profit Target Per Week:

$ ____

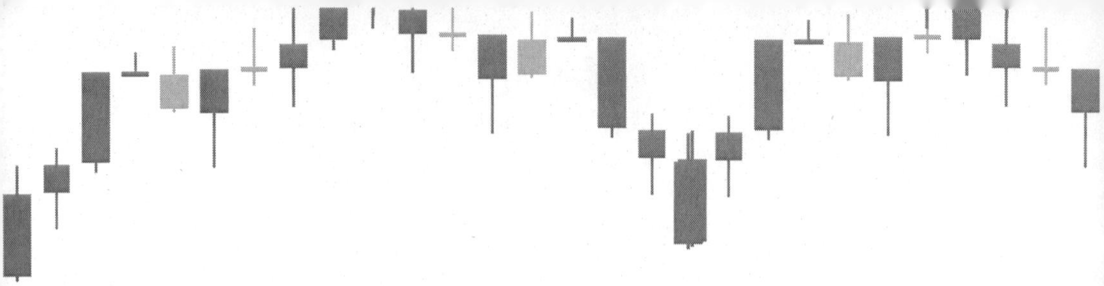

TRADING EMOTIONS

SCARED TIRED SAD HAPPY EXCITED

Notes

DAILY TRADING LOG

Date	Time	Currency Pair	Buy/Sell	Entry Price	Closing	Trade Size

Reason for Entry	Strategy Used	Trade Size
(pattern, news, signal):		

Reason for Entry (pattern, news, signal):

Strategy Used:

Emotional State When Entering Trade:

What I Learned:

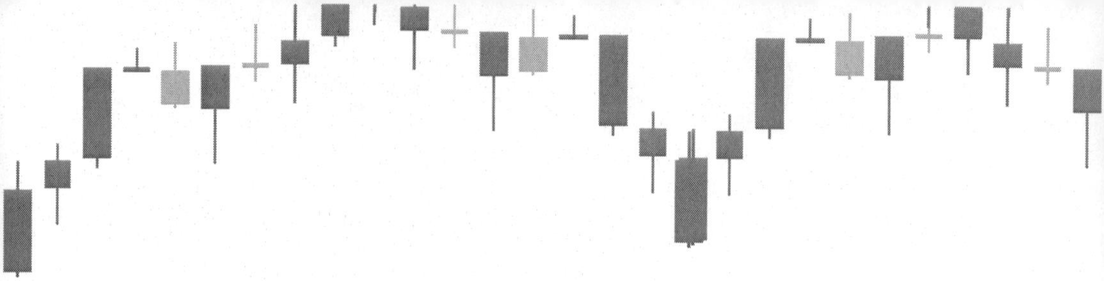

Notes

DAILY TRADING LOG

Date	Time	Currency Pair	Buy/Sell	Entry Price	Closing	Trade Size

Reason for Entry	Strategy Used	Trade Size
(pattern, news, signal):		

Reason for Entry (pattern, news, signal):

Strategy Used:

Emotional State When Entering Trade:

What I Learned:

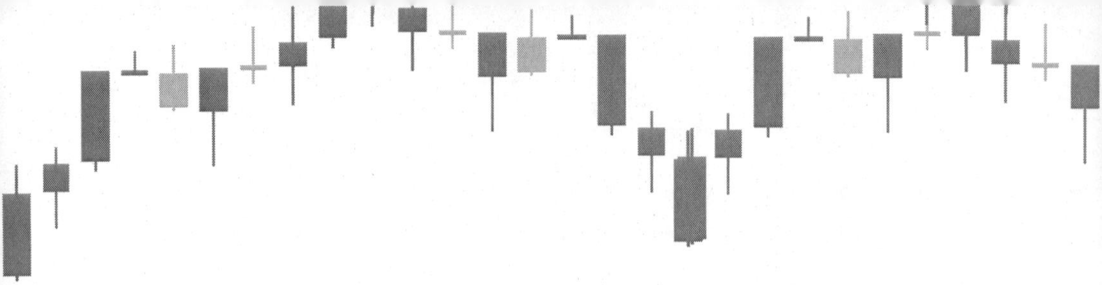

Notes

DAILY TRADING LOG

Date	Time	Currency Pair	Buy/Sell	Entry Price	Closing	Trade Size

Reason for Entry	Strategy Used	Trade Size
(pattern, news, signal):		

Reason for Entry (pattern, news, signal):

Strategy Used:

Emotional State When Entering Trade:

What I Learned:

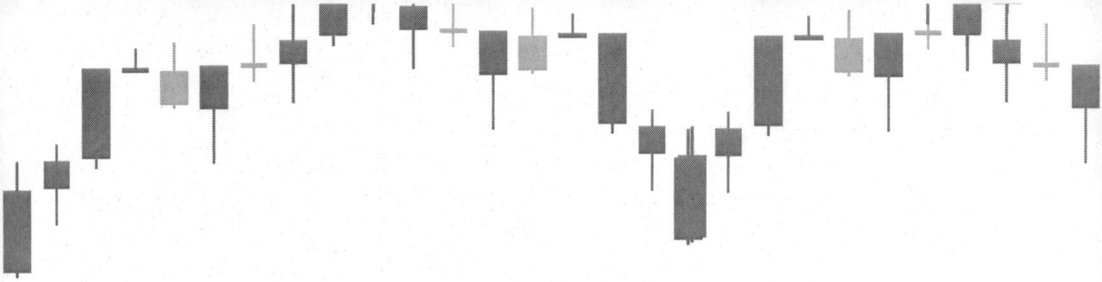

Notes

DAILY TRADING LOG

Date	Time	Currency Pair	Buy/Sell	Entry Price	Closing	Trade Size

Reason for Entry	Strategy Used	Trade Size
(pattern, news, signal):		

Reason for Entry (pattern, news, signal):

Strategy Used:

Emotional State When Entering Trade:

What I Learned:

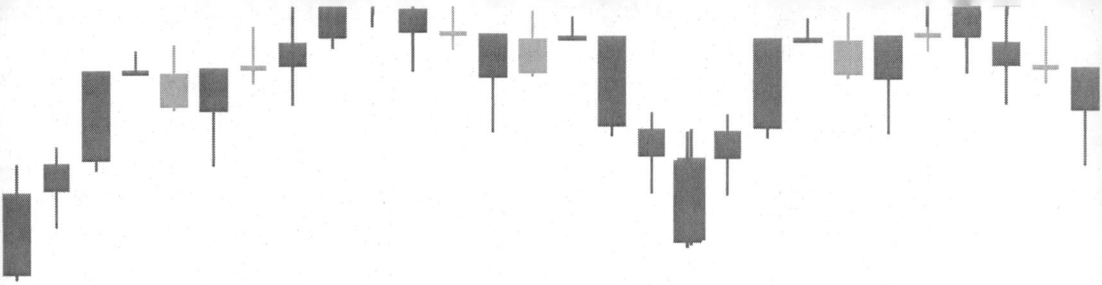

Notes

DAILY TRADING LOG

Date	Time	Currency Pair	Buy/Sell	Entry Price	Closing	Trade Size

Reason for Entry	Strategy Used	Trade Size
(pattern, news, signal):		

Reason for Entry (pattern, news, signal):

Strategy Used:

Emotional State When Entering Trade:

What I Learned:

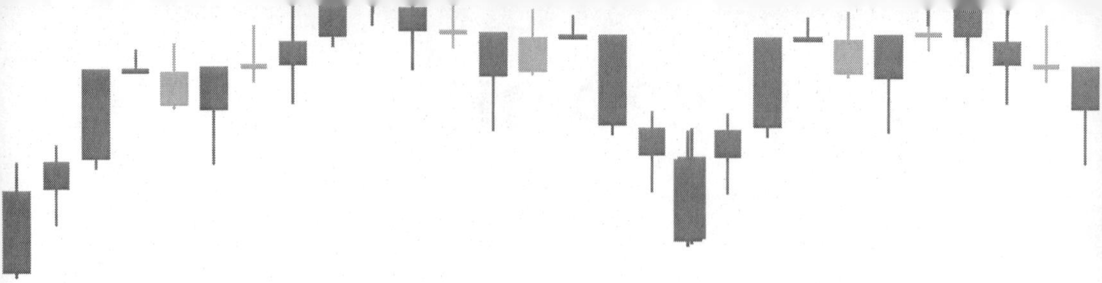

Notes

Weekly Review & Reflection

Weekly Overview

Total Trades Taken: _____ Wins: ___________

Win/Loss Ratio: _________ Win/Loss Prólc

My Biggest Win This Week:

____

____

____

My Biggest Loss This Week:

____

____

Top 3 Lessons Learned:

1. ____
2. ____
3. ____

One Improvement I'll Make Next Week:

____

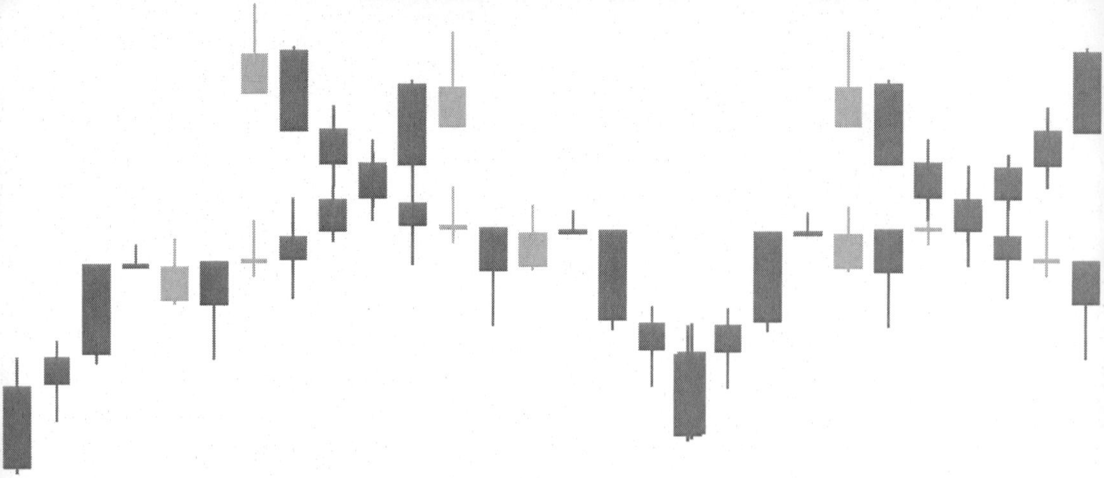

Notes

MY TRADING PLAN

Define Your Personal Trading Blueprint

Successful traders don't rely on luck– they follow a clear, consistent plan. Use this page to set your rules and stick to them.

My Trading Style (check all that apply):

- ☐ Scalping
- ☐ Day Trading
- ☐ Swing Trading
- ☐ Position Trading

My Preferred Currency Pairs:

____

My Maximum Daily Loss Limit:

$ ______________________________

My Profit Target Per Week:

$ ______________________________

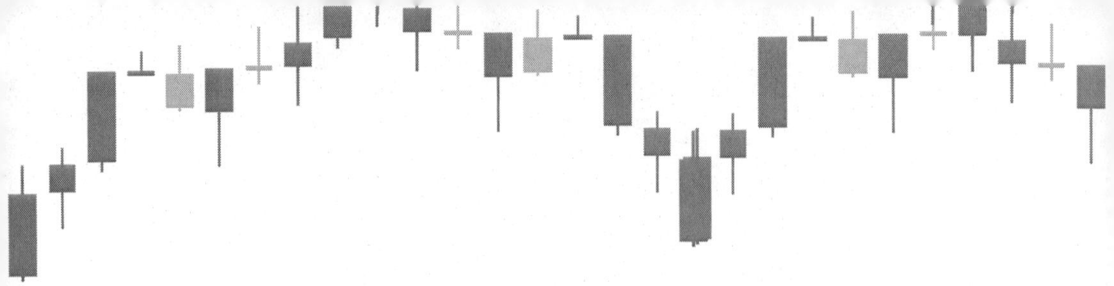

TRADING EMOTIONS

SCARED TIRED SAD HAPPY EXCITED

Notes

DAILY TRADING LOG

Date	Time	Currency Pair	Buy/Sell	Entry Price	Closing	Trade Size

Reason for Entry	Strategy Used	Trade Size
(pattern, news, signal):		

Reason for Entry (pattern, news, signal):

Strategy Used:

Emotional State When Entering Trade:

What I Learned:

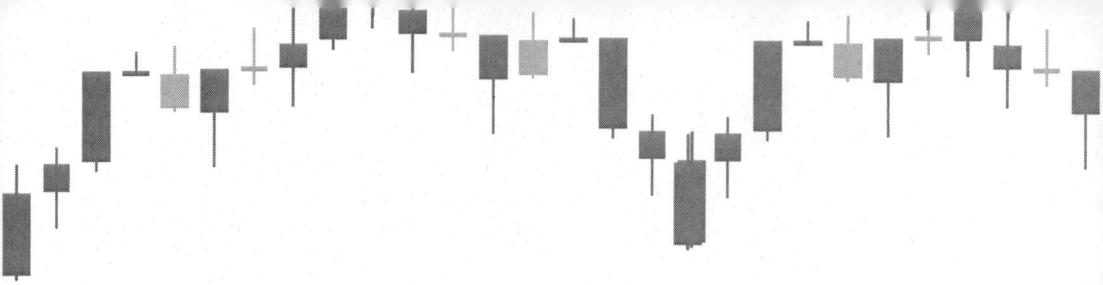

Notes

DAILY TRADING LOG

Date	Time	Currency Pair	Buy/Sell	Entry Price	Closing	Trade Size

Reason for Entry	Strategy Used	Trade Size
(pattern, news, signal):		

Reason for Entry (pattern, news, signal):

Strategy Used:

Emotional State When Entering Trade:

What I Learned:

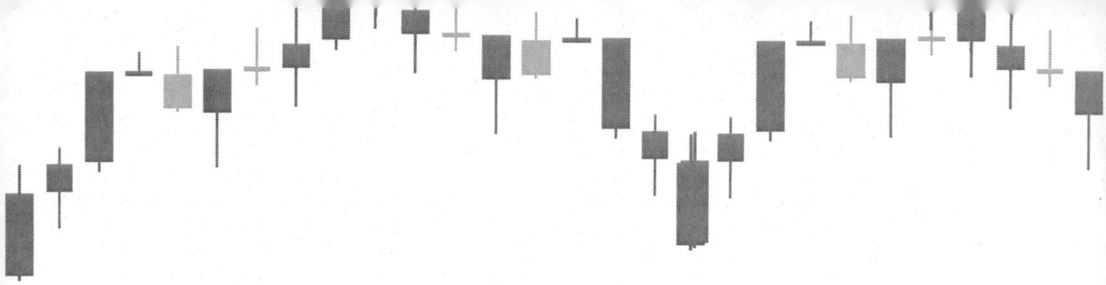

Notes

DAILY TRADING LOG

Date	Time	Currency Pair	Buy/Sell	Entry Price	Closing	Trade Size

Reason for Entry	Strategy Used	Trade Size
(pattern, news, signal):		

Reason for Entry (pattern, news, signal):

Strategy Used:

Emotional State When Entering Trade:

What I Learned:

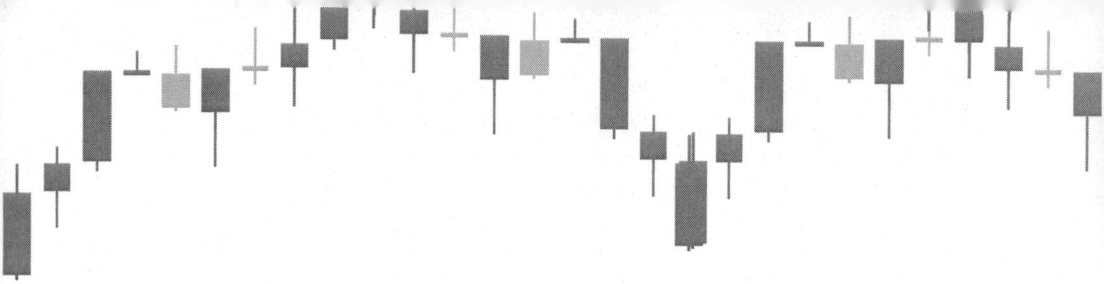

Notes

DAILY TRADING LOG

Date	Time	Currency Pair	Buy/Sell	Entry Price	Closing	Trade Size

Reason for Entry	Strategy Used	Trade Size
(pattern, news, signal):		

Reason for Entry (pattern, news, signal):

Strategy Used:

Emotional State When Entering Trade:

What I Learned:

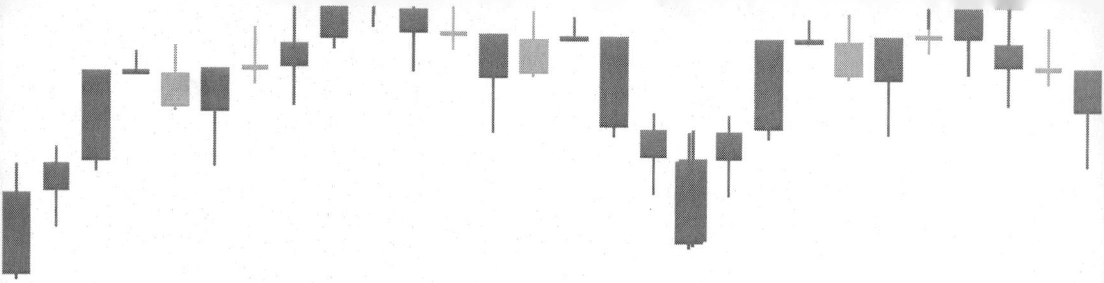

Notes

DAILY TRADING LOG

Date	Time	Currency Pair	Buy/Sell	Entry Price	Closing	Trade Size

Reason for Entry	Strategy Used	Trade Size
(pattern, news, signal):		

Reason for Entry (pattern, news, signal):

Strategy Used:

Emotional State When Entering Trade:

What I Learned:

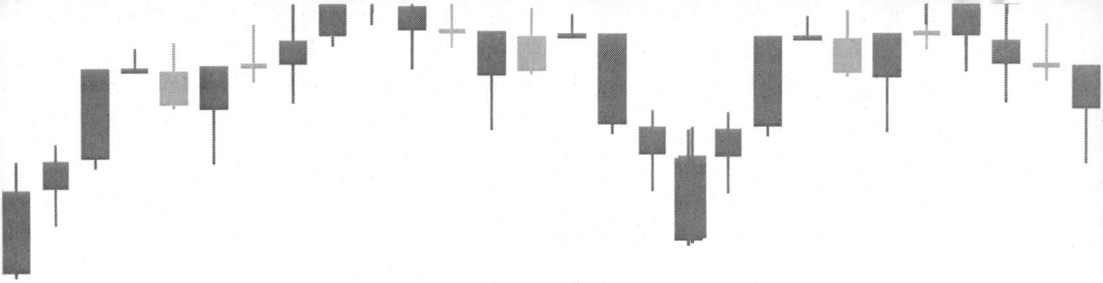

Notes

Weekly Review & Reflection

Weekly Overview

Total Trades Taken: _____ Wins: ___________

Win/Loss Ratio: _________ Win/Loss Prólc

My Biggest Win This Week:

____

____

____

My Biggest Loss This Week:

____

____

Top 3 Lessons Learned:

1. ____
2. ____
3. ____

One Improvement I'll Make Next Week:

____

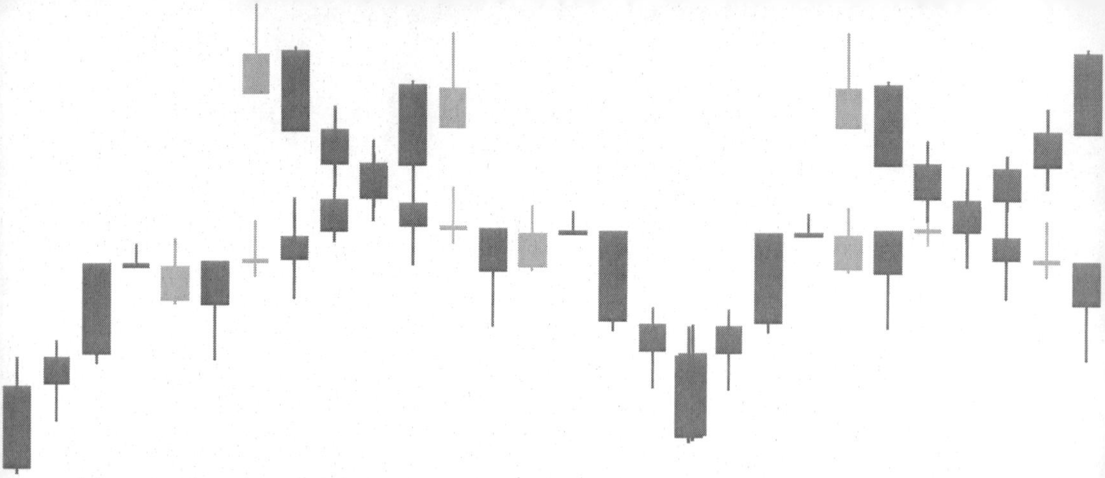

Notes

PROFIT & LOSS MONTHLY SUMMARY

Date	Income	Expenses	Net Profit/Loss

Growth Tracker

What helped me stay disciplined this month?

Where did I break my rules?

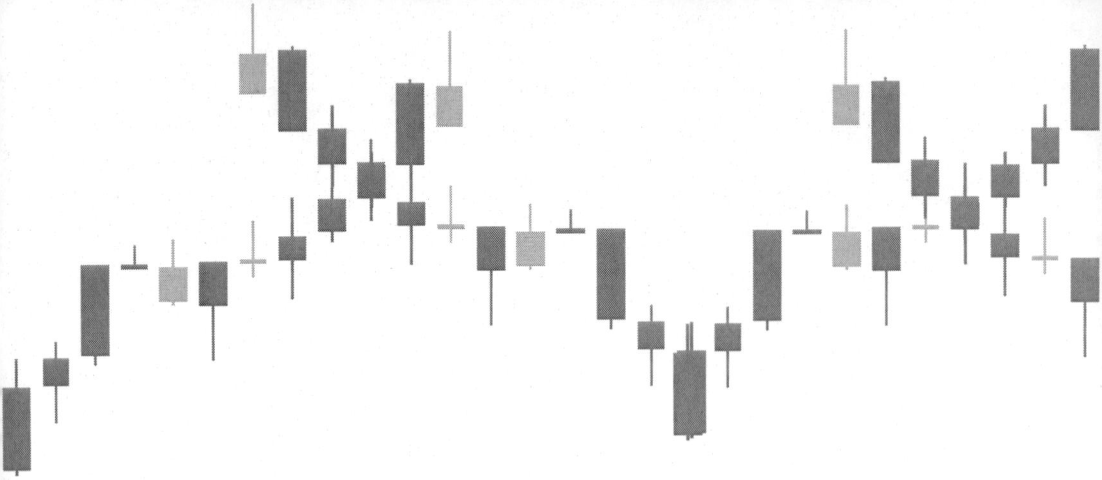

Notes

MY TRADING PLAN

Define Your Personal Trading Blueprint

Successful traders don't rely on luck– they follow a clear, consistent plan. Use this page to set your rules and stick to them.

My Trading Style (check all that apply):

- ☐ Scalping
- ☐ Day Trading
- ☐ Swing Trading
- ☐ Position Trading

My Preferred Currency Pairs:

____

My Maximum Daily Loss Limit:

$ ____

My Profit Target Per Week:

$ ____

TRADING EMOTIONS

SCARED TIRED SAD HAPPY EXCITED

Notes

DAILY TRADING LOG

Date	Time	Currency Pair	Buy/Sell	Entry Price	Closing	Trade Size

Reason for Entry	Strategy Used	Trade Size
(pattern, news, signal):		

Reason for Entry (pattern, news, signal):

Strategy Used:

Emotional State When Entering Trade:

What I Learned:

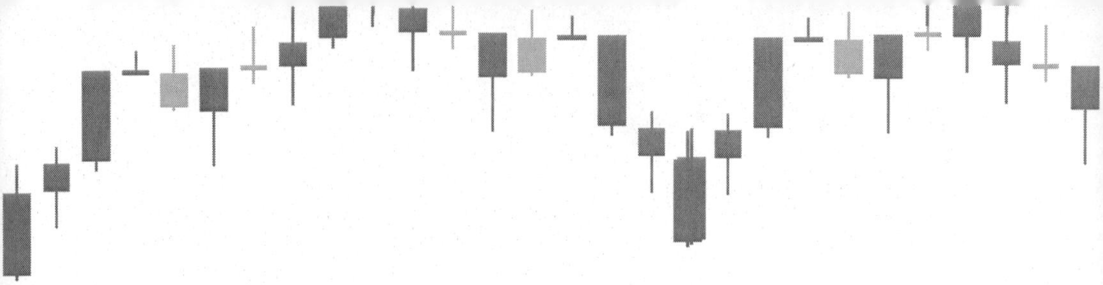

Notes

DAILY TRADING LOG

Date	Time	Currency Pair	Buy/Sell	Entry Price	Closing	Trade Size

Reason for Entry	Strategy Used	Trade Size
(pattern, news, signal):		

Reason for Entry (pattern, news, signal):

Strategy Used:

Emotional State When Entering Trade:

What I Learned:

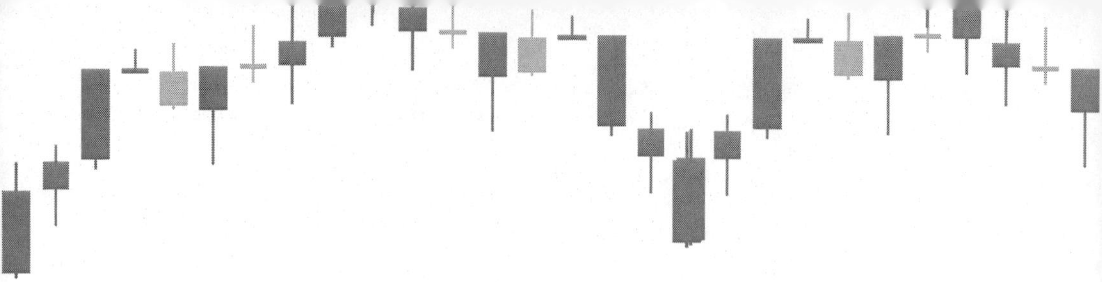

Notes

DAILY TRADING LOG

Date	Time	Currency Pair	Buy/Sell	Entry Price	Closing	Trade Size

Reason for Entry	Strategy Used	Trade Size
(pattern, news, signal):		

Reason for Entry (pattern, news, signal):

Strategy Used:

Emotional State When Entering Trade:

What I Learned:

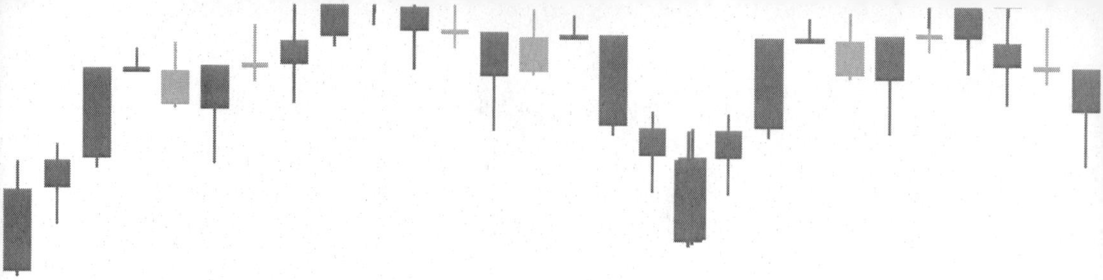

Notes

DAILY TRADING LOG

Date	Time	Currency Pair	Buy/Sell	Entry Price	Closing	Trade Size

Reason for Entry	Strategy Used	Trade Size
(pattern, news, signal):		

Reason for Entry (pattern, news, signal):

Strategy Used:

Emotional State When Entering Trade:

What I Learned:

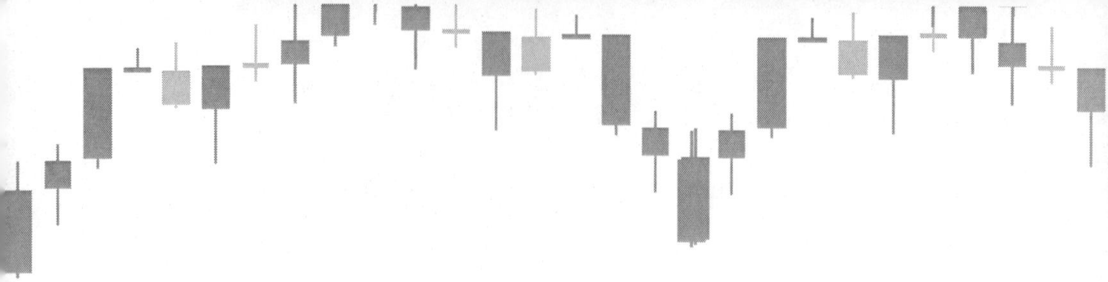

Notes

DAILY TRADING LOG

Date	Time	Currency Pair	Buy/Sell	Entry Price	Closing	Trade Size

Reason for Entry	Strategy Used	Trade Size
(pattern, news, signal):		

Reason for Entry (pattern, news, signal):

Strategy Used:

Emotional State When Entering Trade:

What I Learned:

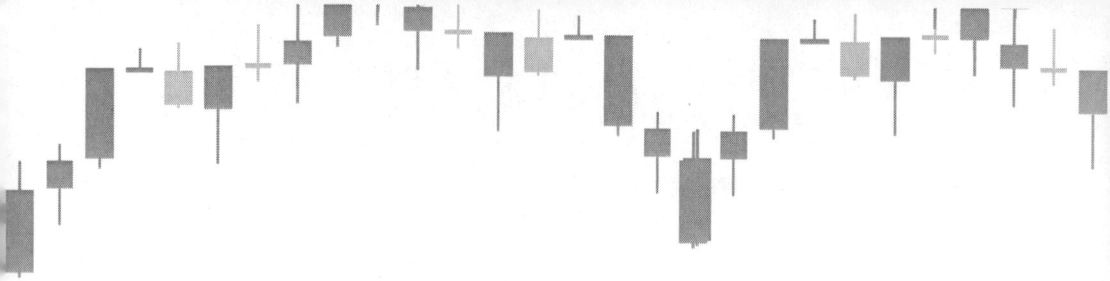

Notes

Weekly Review & Reflection

Weekly Overview

Total Trades Taken: _____ Wins: ___________

Win/Loss Ratio: _________ Win/Loss Prólc

My Biggest Win This Week:

____

____

____

My Biggest Loss This Week:

____

____

Top 3 Lessons Learned:

1. ____
2. ____
3. ____

One Improvement I'll Make Next Week:

____

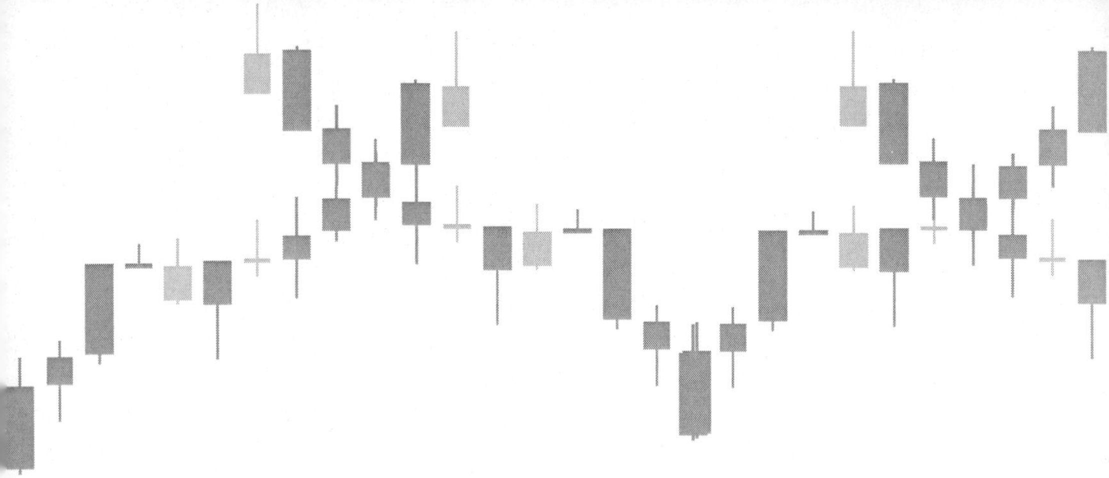

Notes

MY TRADING PLAN

Define Your Personal Trading Blueprint

Successful traders don't rely on luck– they follow a clear, consistent plan. Use this page to set your rules and stick to them.

My Trading Style (check all that apply):

- ☐ Scalping
- ☐ Day Trading
- ☐ Swing Trading
- ☐ Position Trading

My Preferred Currency Pairs:

____

My Maximum Daily Loss Limit:

$ ______________________________________

My Profit Target Per Week:

$ ______________________________________

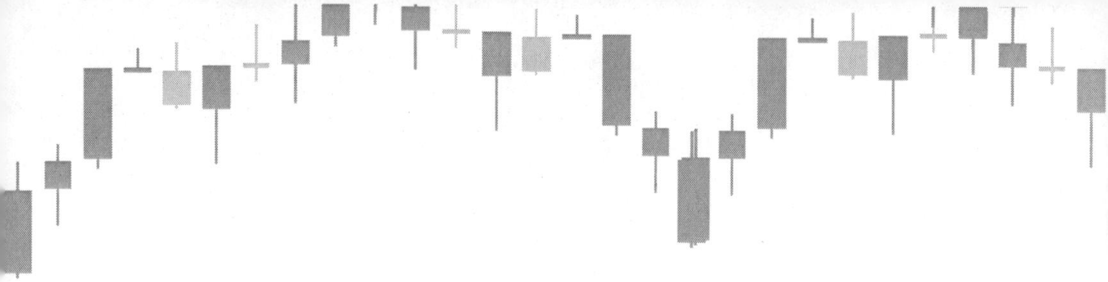

TRADING EMOTIONS

SCARED TIRED SAD HAPPY EXCITED

Notes

DAILY TRADING LOG

Date	Time	Currency Pair	Buy/Sell	Entry Price	Closing	Trade Size

Reason for Entry	Strategy Used	Trade Size
(pattern, news, signal):		

Reason for Entry (pattern, news, signal):

Strategy Used:

Emotional State When Entering Trade:

What I Learned:

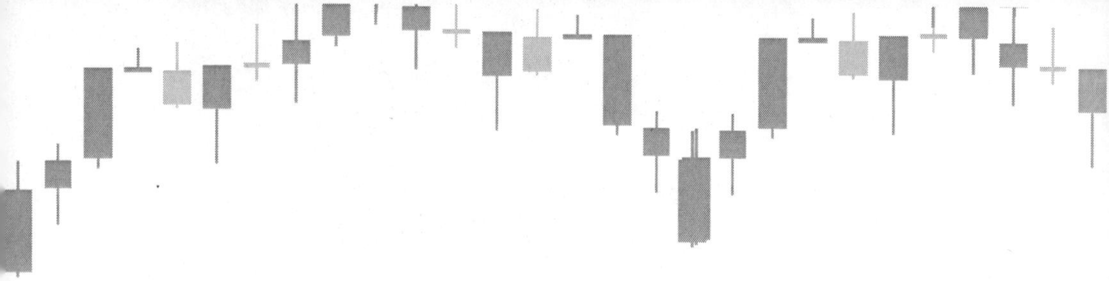

Notes

DAILY TRADING LOG

Date	Time	Currency Pair	Buy/Sell	Entry Price	Closing	Trade Size

Reason for Entry	Strategy Used	Trade Size
(pattern, news, signal):		

Reason for Entry (pattern, news, signal):

Strategy Used:

Emotional State When Entering Trade:

What I Learned:

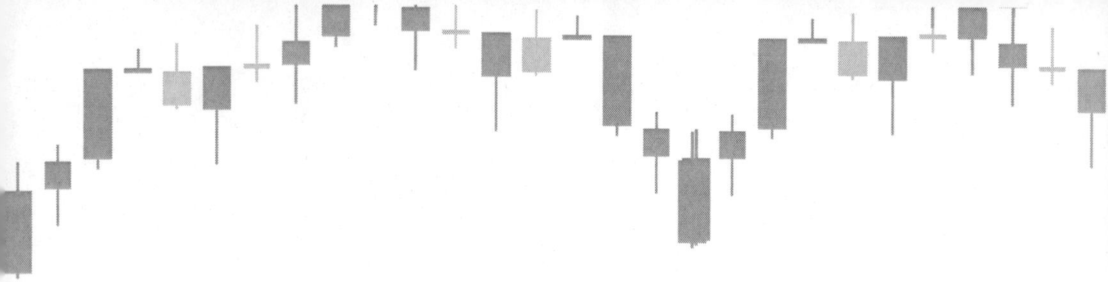

Notes

DAILY TRADING LOG

Date	Time	Currency Pair	Buy/Sell	Entry Price	Closing	Trade Size

Reason for Entry	Strategy Used	Trade Size
(pattern, news, signal):		

Reason for Entry (pattern, news, signal):

Strategy Used:

Emotional State When Entering Trade:

What I Learned:

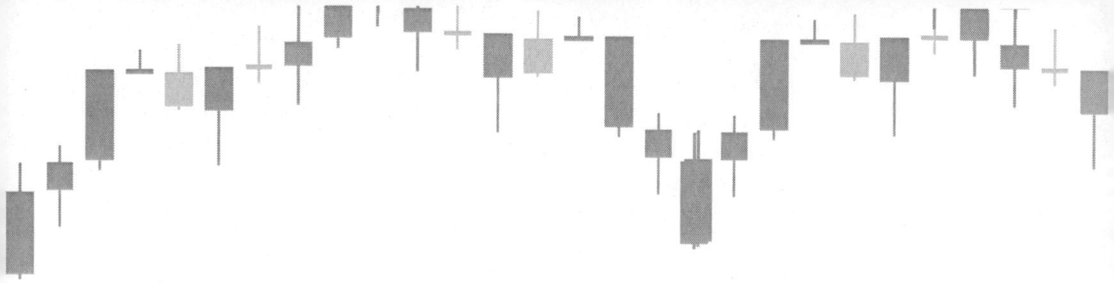

Notes

DAILY TRADING LOG

Date	Time	Currency Pair	Buy/Sell	Entry Price	Closing	Trade Size

Reason for Entry	Strategy Used	Trade Size
(pattern, news, signal):		

Reason for Entry (pattern, news, signal):

Strategy Used:

Emotional State When Entering Trade:

What I Learned:

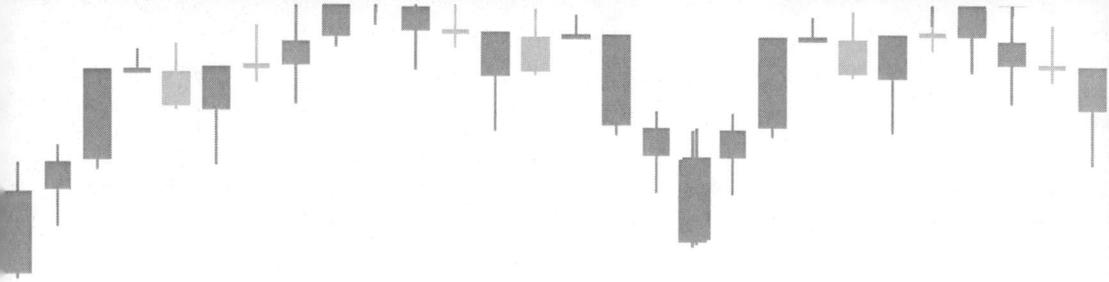

Notes

DAILY TRADING LOG

Date	Time	Currency Pair	Buy/Sell	Entry Price	Closing	Trade Size

Reason for Entry	Strategy Used	Trade Size
(pattern, news, signal):		

Reason for Entry (pattern, news, signal):

Strategy Used:

Emotional State When Entering Trade:

What I Learned:

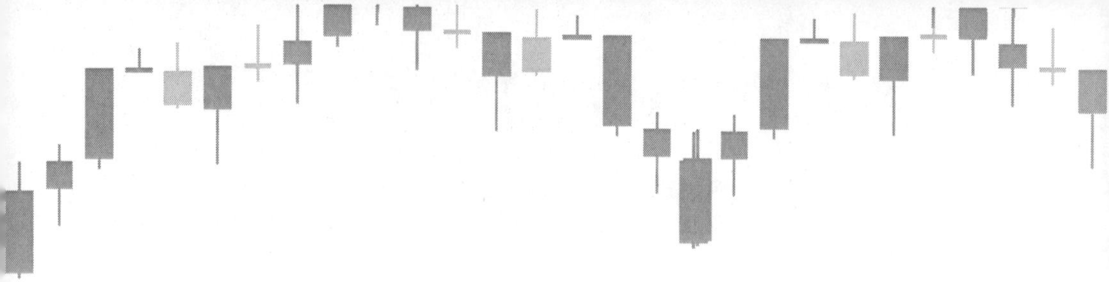

Notes

Weekly Review & Reflection

Weekly Overview

Total Trades Taken: _____ Wins: ___________

Win/Loss Ratio: _________ Win/Loss Prólc

My Biggest Win This Week:

____

____

____

My Biggest Loss This Week:

____

____

Top 3 Lessons Learned:

1. ____
2. ____
3. ____

One Improvement I'll Make Next Week:

____

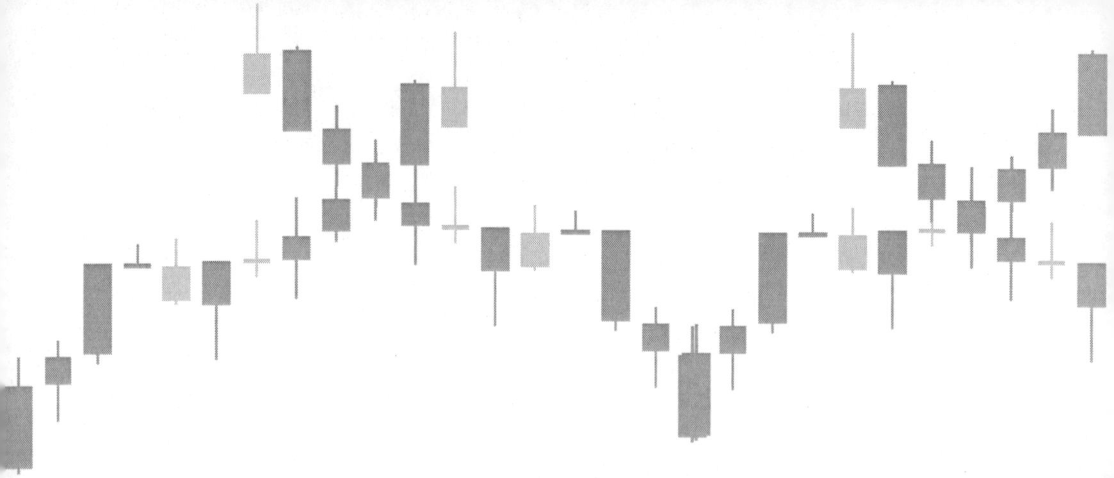

Notes

MY TRADING PLAN

Define Your Personal Trading Blueprint

Successful traders don't rely on luck– they follow a clear, consistent plan. Use this page to set your rules and stick to them.

My Trading Style (check all that apply):

- ☐ Scalping
- ☐ Day Trading
- ☐ Swing Trading
- ☐ Position Trading

My Preferred Currency Pairs:

____

My Maximum Daily Loss Limit:

$ ______________________________

My Profit Target Per Week:

$ ______________________________

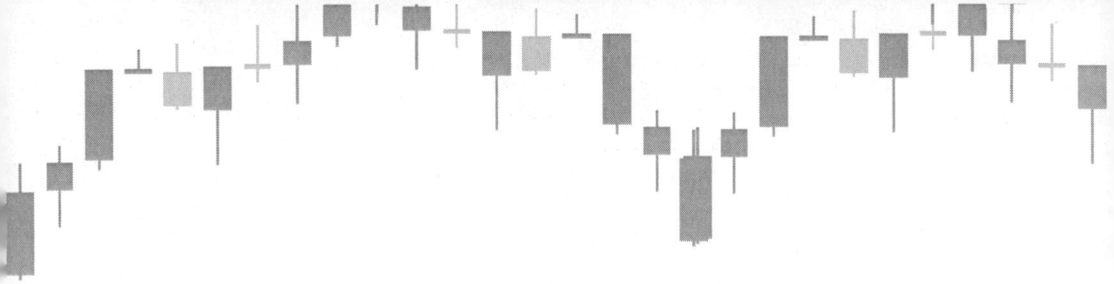

TRADING EMOTIONS

SCARED TIRED SAD HAPPY EXCITED

Notes

DAILY TRADING LOG

Date	Time	Currency Pair	Buy/Sell	Entry Price	Closing	Trade Size

Reason for Entry	Strategy Used	Trade Size
(pattern, news, signal):		

Reason for Entry (pattern, news, signal):

Strategy Used:

Emotional State When Entering Trade:

What I Learned:

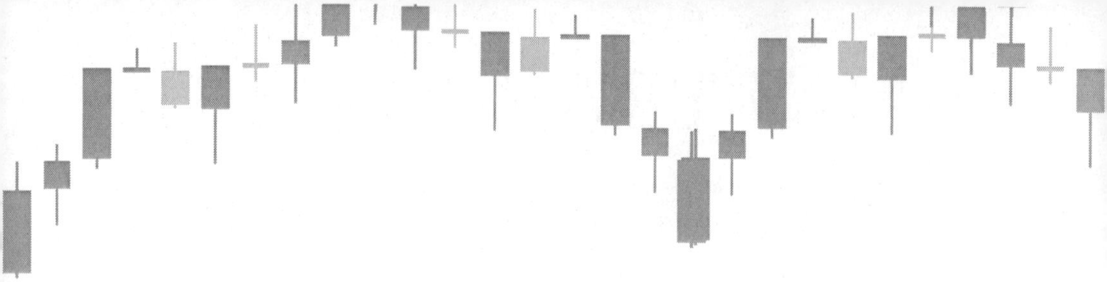

Notes

DAILY TRADING LOG

Date	Time	Currency Pair	Buy/Sell	Entry Price	Closing	Trade Size

Reason for Entry	Strategy Used	Trade Size
(pattern, news, signal):		

Reason for Entry (pattern, news, signal):

Strategy Used:

Emotional State When Entering Trade:

What I Learned:

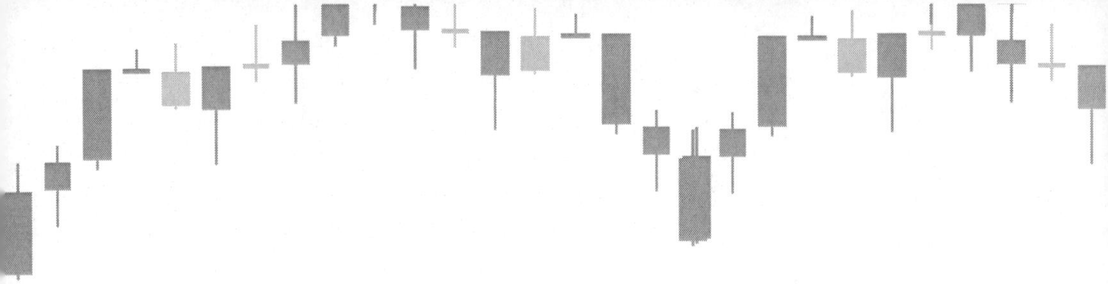

Notes

DAILY TRADING LOG

Date	Time	Currency Pair	Buy/Sell	Entry Price	Closing	Trade Size

Reason for Entry	Strategy Used	Trade Size
(pattern, news, signal):		

Reason for Entry (pattern, news, signal):

Strategy Used:

Emotional State When Entering Trade:

What I Learned:

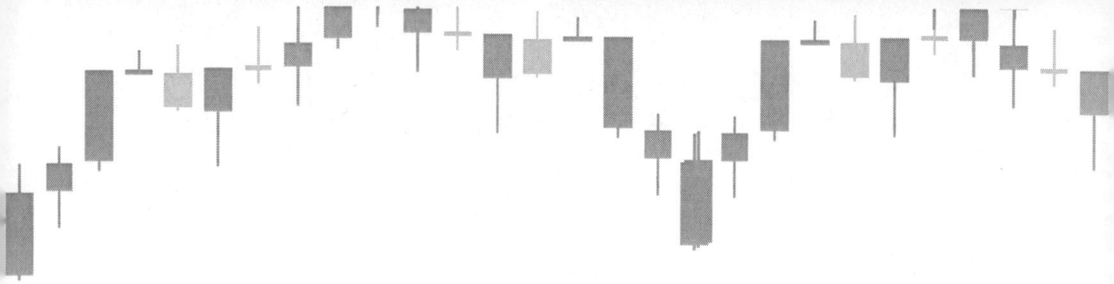

Notes

DAILY TRADING LOG

Date	Time	Currency Pair	Buy/Sell	Entry Price	Closing	Trade Size

Reason for Entry	Strategy Used	Trade Size
(pattern, news, signal):		

Reason for Entry (pattern, news, signal):

Strategy Used:

Emotional State When Entering Trade:

What I Learned:

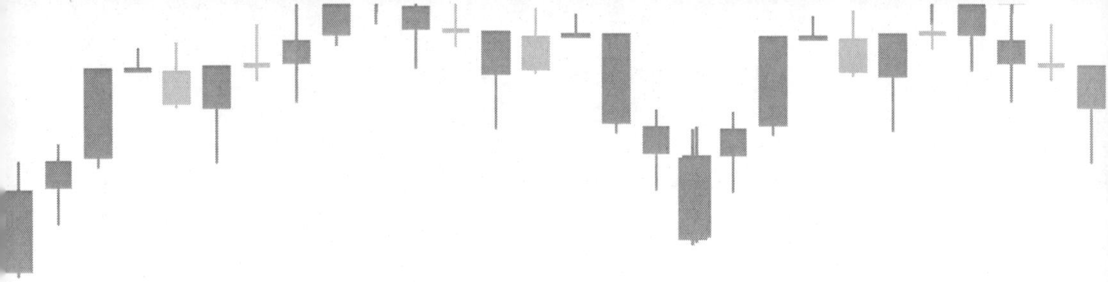

Notes

DAILY TRADING LOG

Date	Time	Currency Pair	Buy/Sell	Entry Price	Closing	Trade Size

Reason for Entry	Strategy Used	Trade Size
(pattern, news, signal):		

Reason for Entry (pattern, news, signal):

Strategy Used:

Emotional State When Entering Trade:

What I Learned:

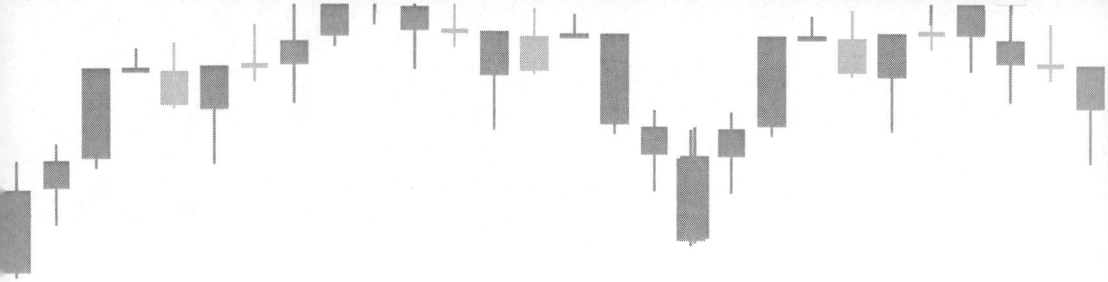

Notes

Weekly Review & Reflection

Weekly Overview

Total Trades Taken: _____ Wins: ___________

Win/Loss Ratio: _________ Win/Loss Prólc

My Biggest Win This Week:

____

____

____

My Biggest Loss This Week:

____

____

Top 3 Lessons Learned:

1. ______________________________
2. ______________________________
3. ______________________________

One Improvement I'll Make Next Week:

____

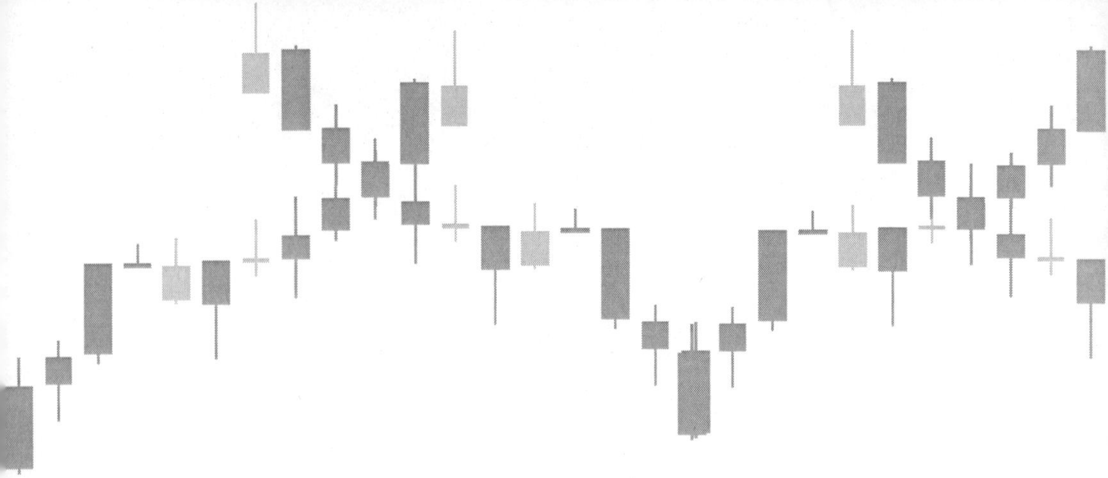

Notes

MY TRADING PLAN

Define Your Personal Trading Blueprint

Successful traders don't rely on luck– they follow a clear, consistent plan. Use this page to set your rules and stick to them.

My Trading Style (check all that apply):

- ☐ Scalping
- ☐ Day Trading
- ☐ Swing Trading
- ☐ Position Trading

My Preferred Currency Pairs:

____

My Maximum Daily Loss Limit:

$ ______________________________

My Profit Target Per Week:

$ ______________________________

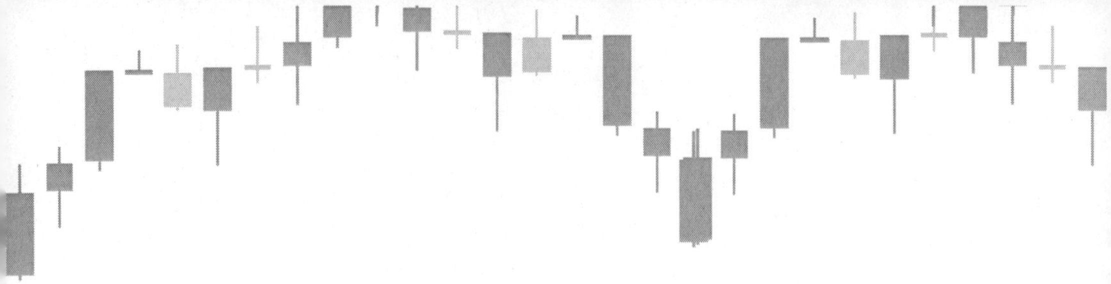

TRADING EMOTIONS

SCARED TIRED SAD HAPPY EXCITED

Notes

DAILY TRADING LOG

Date	Time	Currency Pair	Buy/Sell	Entry Price	Closing	Trade Size

Reason for Entry	Strategy Used	Trade Size
(pattern, news, signal):		

Reason for Entry (pattern, news, signal):

Strategy Used:

Emotional State When Entering Trade:

What I Learned:

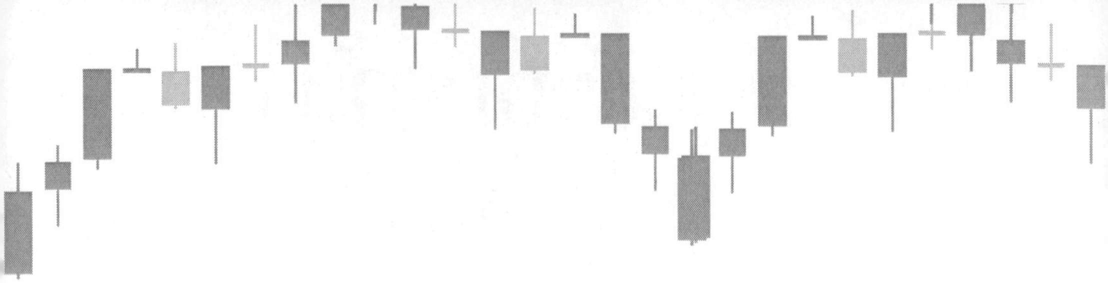

Notes

DAILY TRADING LOG

Date	Time	Currency Pair	Buy/Sell	Entry Price	Closing	Trade Size

Reason for Entry	Strategy Used	Trade Size
(pattern, news, signal):		

Reason for Entry (pattern, news, signal):

Strategy Used:

Emotional State When Entering Trade:

What I Learned:

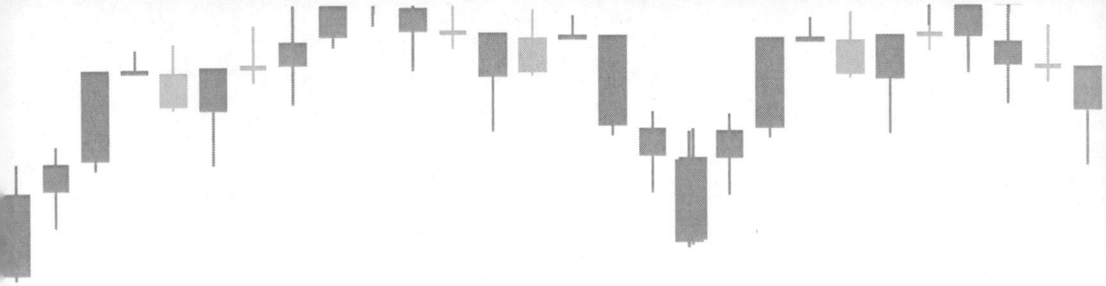

Notes

DAILY TRADING LOG

Date	Time	Currency Pair	Buy/Sell	Entry Price	Closing	Trade Size

Reason for Entry	Strategy Used	Trade Size
(pattern, news, signal):		

Reason for Entry (pattern, news, signal):

Strategy Used:

Emotional State When Entering Trade:

What I Learned:

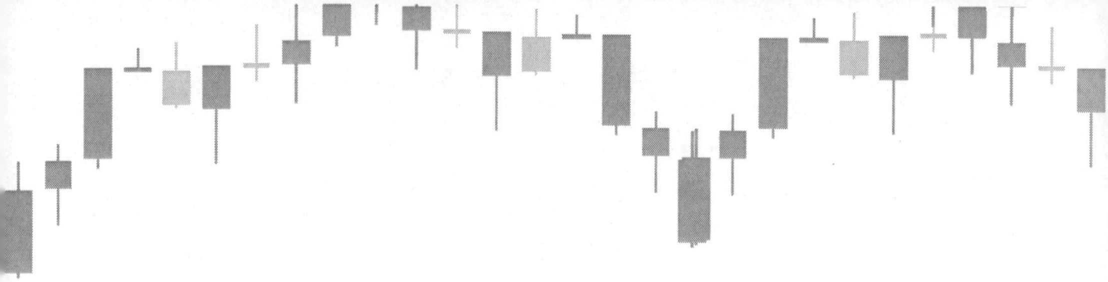

Notes

DAILY TRADING LOG

Date	Time	Currency Pair	Buy/Sell	Entry Price	Closing	Trade Size

Reason for Entry	Strategy Used	Trade Size
(pattern, news, signal):		

Reason for Entry (pattern, news, signal):

Strategy Used:

Emotional State When Entering Trade:

What I Learned:

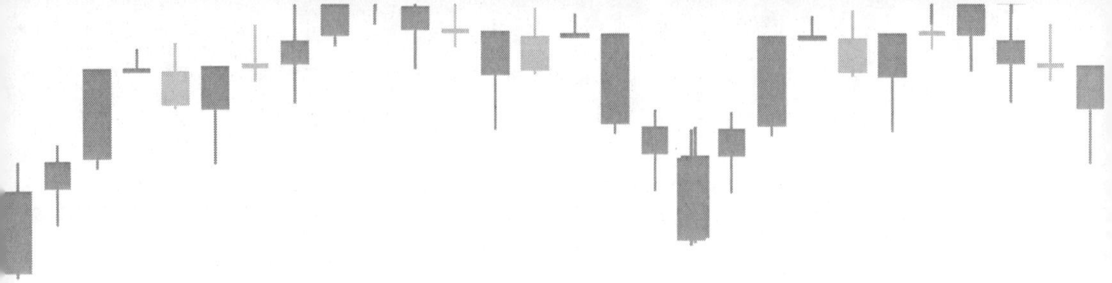

Notes

DAILY TRADING LOG

Date	Time	Currency Pair	Buy/Sell	Entry Price	Closing	Trade Size

Reason for Entry	Strategy Used	Trade Size
(pattern, news, signal):		

Reason for Entry (pattern, news, signal):

Strategy Used:

Emotional State When Entering Trade:

What I Learned:

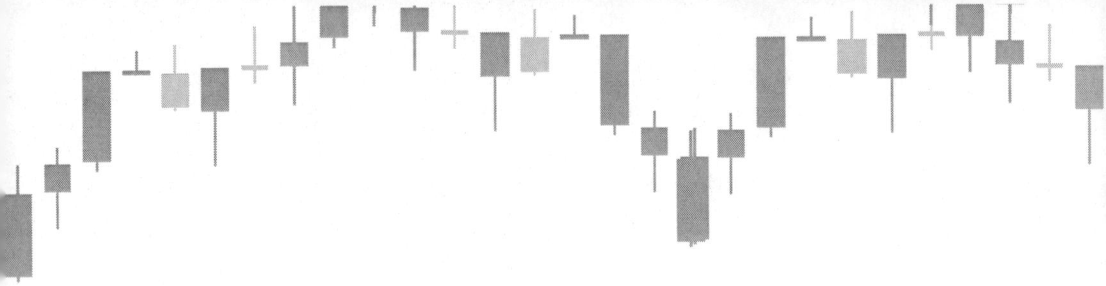

Notes

Weekly Review & Reflection

Weekly Overview

Total Trades Taken: _____ Wins: ___________

Win/Loss Ratio: _________ Win/Loss Prólc

My Biggest Win This Week:

____

____

____

My Biggest Loss This Week:

____

____

3 Top 3 Lessons Learned:

1. ____
2. ____
3. ____

One Improvement I'll Make Next Week:

____

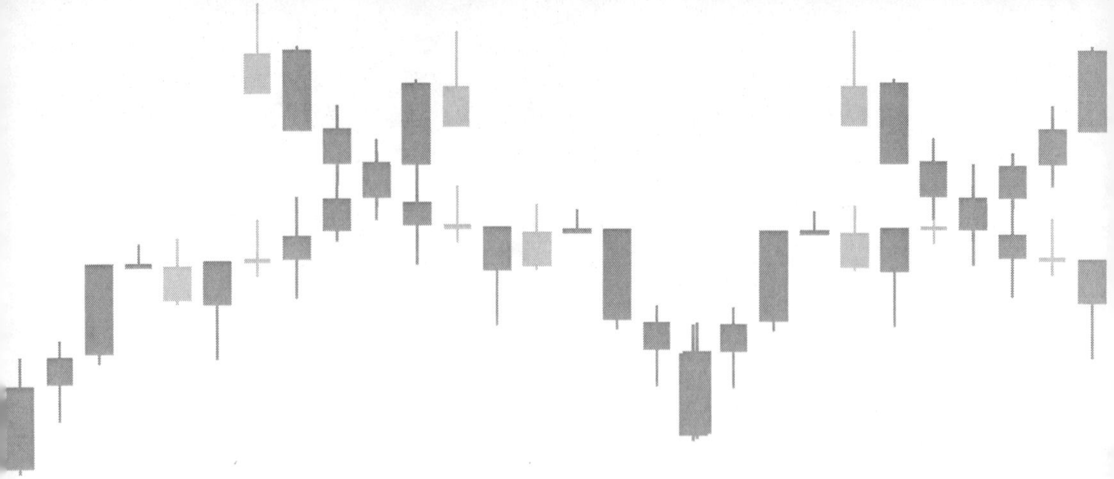

Notes

MY TRADING PLAN

Define Your Personal Trading Blueprint

Successful traders don't rely on luck– they follow a clear, consistent plan. Use this page to set your rules and stick to them.

My Trading Style (check all that apply):

- ☐ Scalping
- ☐ Day Trading
- ☐ Swing Trading
- ☐ Position Trading

My Preferred Currency Pairs:

____

My Maximum Daily Loss Limit:

$ ______________________________

My Profit Target Per Week:

$ ______________________________

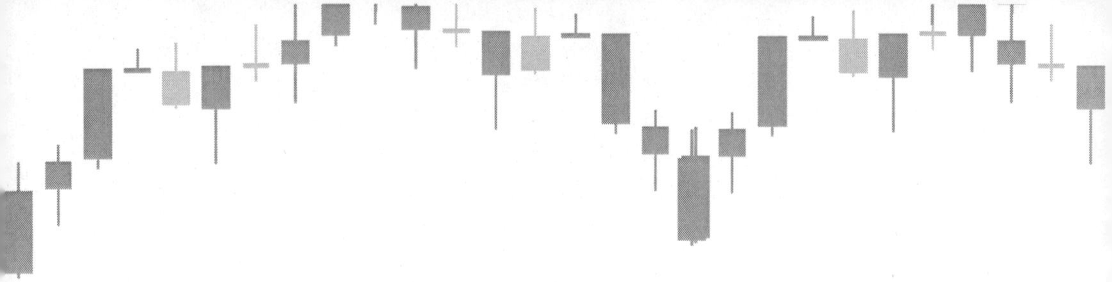

TRADING EMOTIONS

SCARED TIRED SAD HAPPY EXCITED

Notes

DAILY TRADING LOG

Date	Time	Currency Pair	Buy/Sell	Entry Price	Closing	Trade Size

Reason for Entry	Strategy Used	Trade Size
(pattern, news, signal):		

Reason for Entry (pattern, news, signal):

Strategy Used:

Emotional State When Entering Trade:

What I Learned:

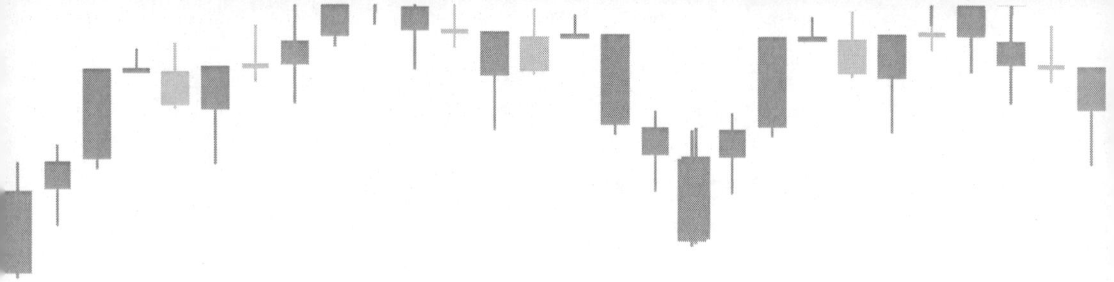

Notes

DAILY TRADING LOG

Date	Time	Currency Pair	Buy/Sell	Entry Price	Closing	Trade Size

Reason for Entry	Strategy Used	Trade Size
(pattern, news, signal):		

Reason for Entry (pattern, news, signal):

Strategy Used:

Emotional State When Entering Trade:

What I Learned:

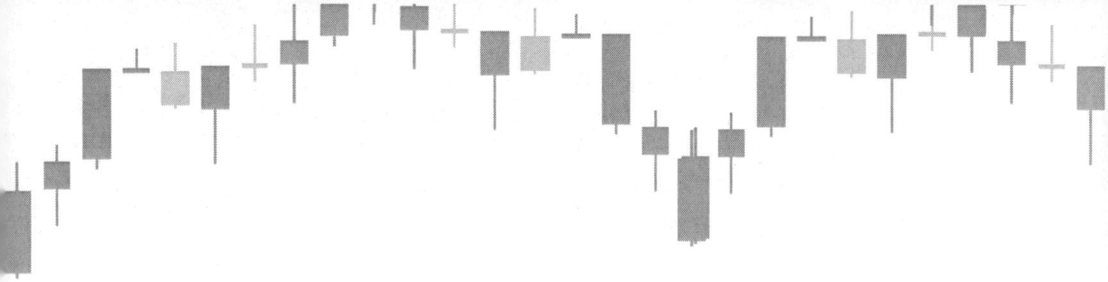

Notes

DAILY TRADING LOG

Date	Time	Currency Pair	Buy/Sell	Entry Price	Closing	Trade Size

Reason for Entry	Strategy Used	Trade Size
(pattern, news, signal):		

Reason for Entry (pattern, news, signal):

Strategy Used:

Emotional State When Entering Trade:

What I Learned:

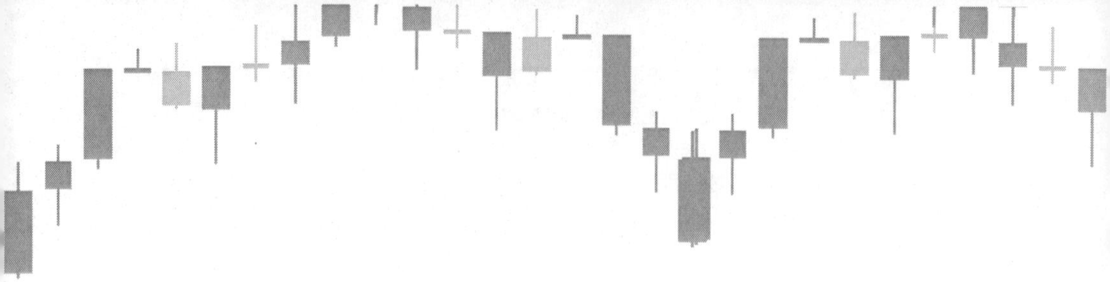

Notes

DAILY TRADING LOG

Date	Time	Currency Pair	Buy/Sell	Entry Price	Closing	Trade Size

Reason for Entry	Strategy Used	Trade Size
(pattern, news, signal):		

Reason for Entry (pattern, news, signal):

Strategy Used:

Emotional State When Entering Trade:

What I Learned:

Notes

DAILY TRADING LOG

Date	Time	Currency Pair	Buy/Sell	Entry Price	Closing	Trade Size

Reason for Entry	Strategy Used	Trade Size
(pattern, news, signal):		

Reason for Entry (pattern, news, signal):

Strategy Used:

Emotional State When Entering Trade:

What I Learned:

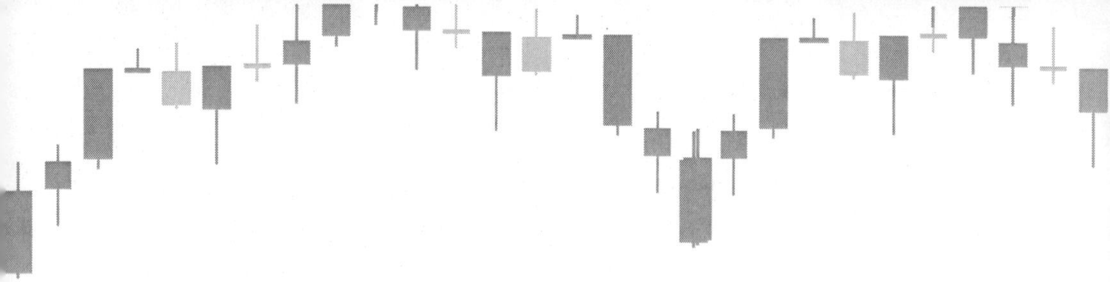

Notes

Weekly Review & Reflection

Weekly Overview

Total Trades Taken: _____ Wins: ___________

Win/Loss Ratio: _________ Win/Loss Prólc

My Biggest Win This Week:

____

____

____

My Biggest Loss This Week:

____

____

Top 3 Lessons Learned:

1. ____
2. ____
3. ____

One Improvement I'll Make Next Week:

____

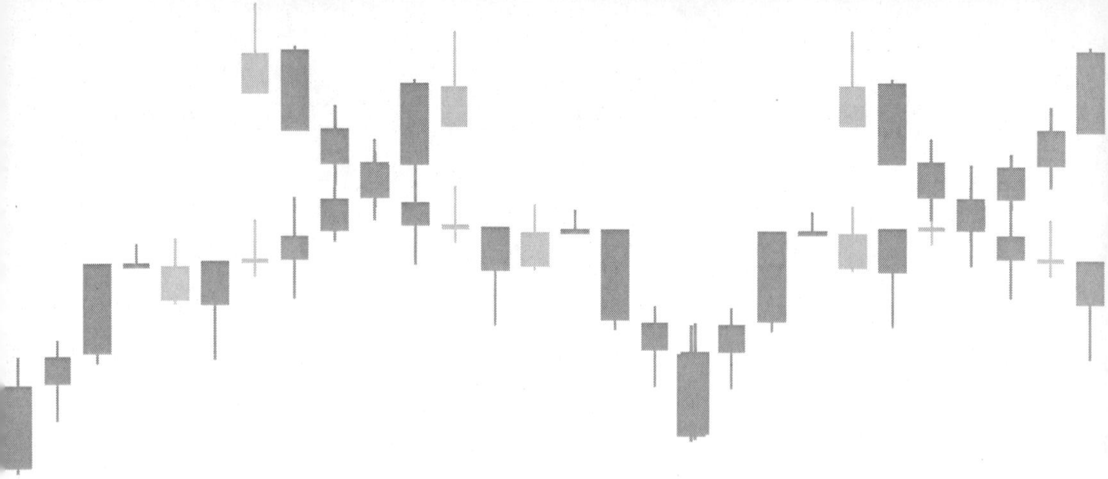

Notes

MY TRADING PLAN

Define Your Personal Trading Blueprint

Successful traders don't rely on luck– they follow a clear, consistent plan. Use this page to set your rules and stick to them.

My Trading Style (check all that apply):

- ☐ Scalping
- ☐ Day Trading
- ☐ Swing Trading
- ☐ Position Trading

My Preferred Currency Pairs:

____

My Maximum Daily Loss Limit:

$ ______________________________

My Profit Target Per Week:

$ ______________________________

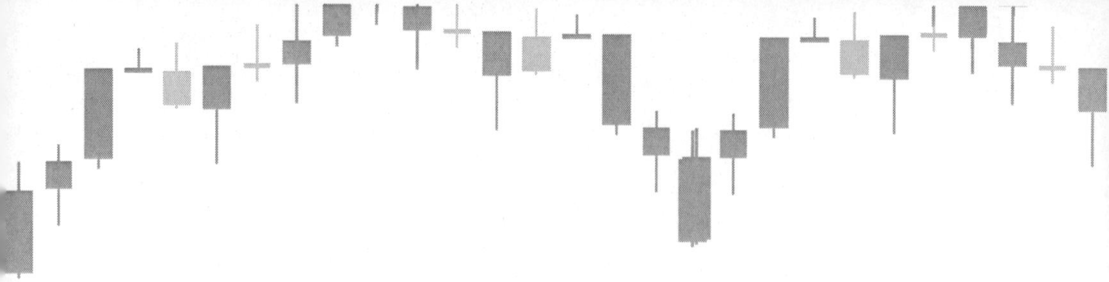

TRADING EMOTIONS

SCARED TIRED SAD HAPPY EXCITED

Notes

DAILY TRADING LOG

Date	Time	Currency Pair	Buy/Sell	Entry Price	Closing	Trade Size

Reason for Entry	Strategy Used	Trade Size
(pattern, news, signal):		

Reason for Entry (pattern, news, signal):

Strategy Used:

Emotional State When Entering Trade:

What I Learned:

Notes

DAILY TRADING LOG

Date	Time	Currency Pair	Buy/Sell	Entry Price	Closing	Trade Size

Reason for Entry	Strategy Used	Trade Size
(pattern, news, signal):		

Reason for Entry (pattern, news, signal):

Strategy Used:

Emotional State When Entering Trade:

What I Learned:

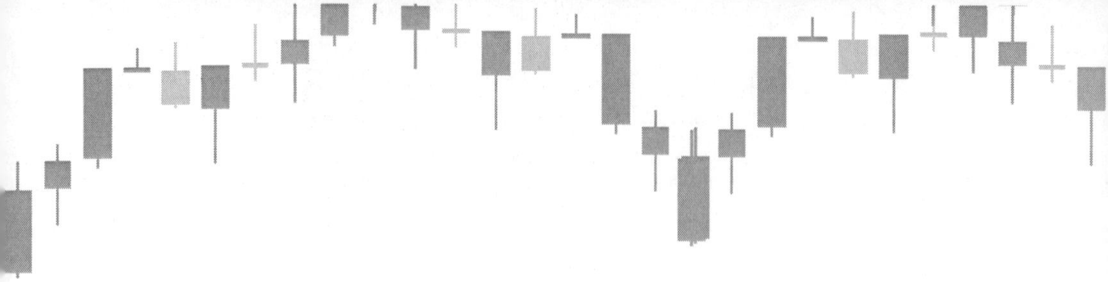

Notes

DAILY TRADING LOG

Date	Time	Currency Pair	Buy/Sell	Entry Price	Closing	Trade Size

Reason for Entry	Strategy Used	Trade Size
(pattern, news, signal):		

Reason for Entry (pattern, news, signal):

Strategy Used:

Emotional State When Entering Trade:

What I Learned:

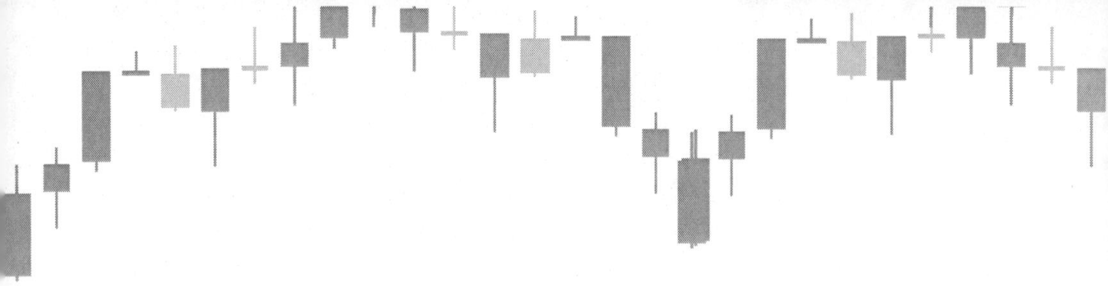

Notes

DAILY TRADING LOG

Date	Time	Currency Pair	Buy/Sell	Entry Price	Closing	Trade Size

Reason for Entry	Strategy Used	Trade Size
(pattern, news, signal):		

Reason for Entry (pattern, news, signal):

Strategy Used:

Emotional State When Entering Trade:

What I Learned:

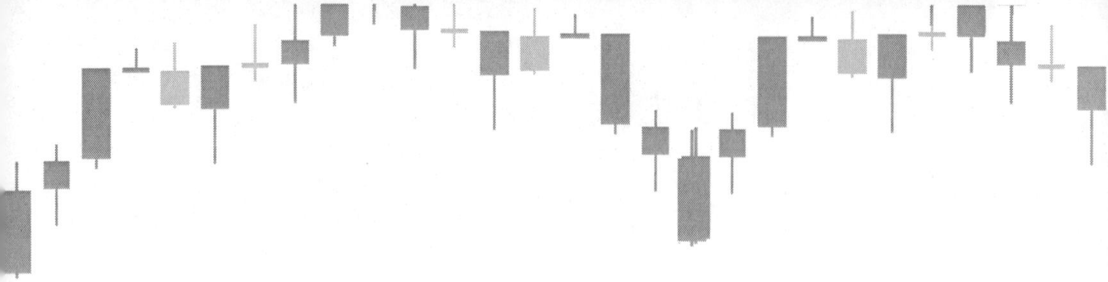

Notes

DAILY TRADING LOG

Date	Time	Currency Pair	Buy/Sell	Entry Price	Closing	Trade Size

Reason for Entry	Strategy Used	Trade Size
(pattern, news, signal):		

Reason for Entry (pattern, news, signal):

Strategy Used:

Emotional State When Entering Trade:

What I Learned:

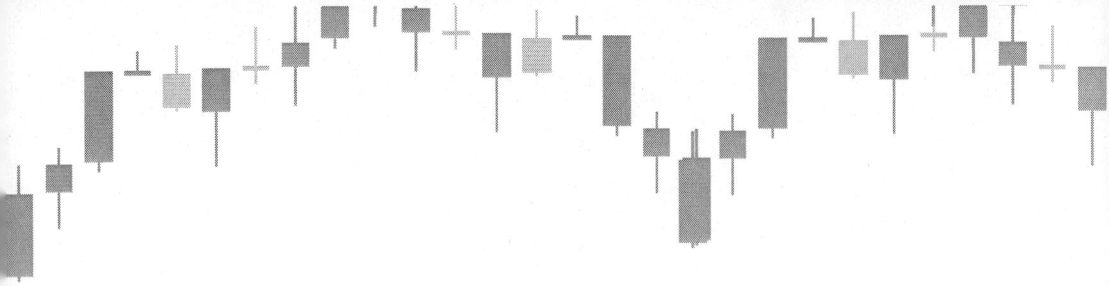

Notes

Weekly Review & Reflection

Weekly Overview

Total Trades Taken: _____ Wins: ___________

Win/Loss Ratio: _________ Win/Loss Prólc

My Biggest Win This Week:

____

____

____

My Biggest Loss This Week:

____

____

Top 3 Lessons Learned:

1. ____
2. ____
3. ____

One Improvement I'll Make Next Week:

____

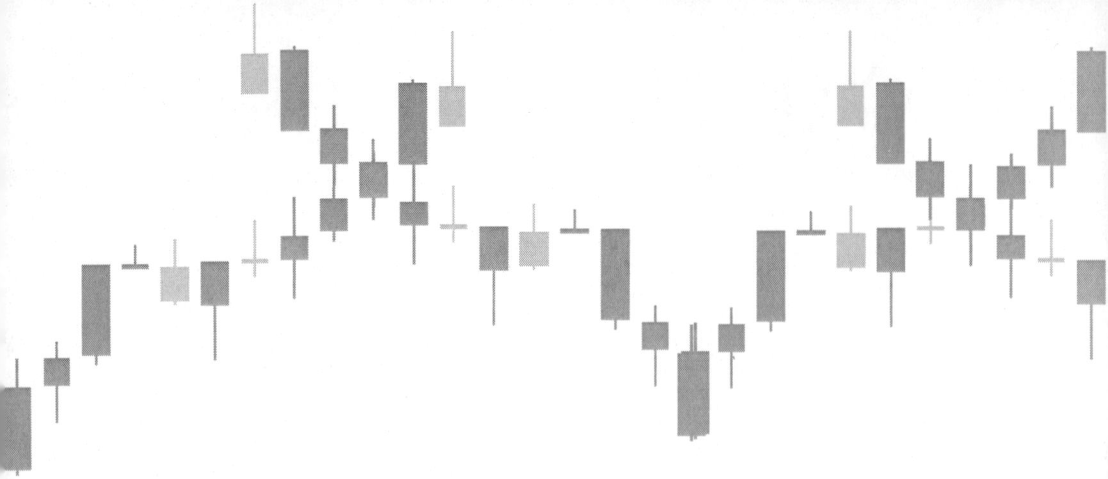

Notes

PROFIT & LOSS MONTHLY SUMMARY

Date	Income	Expenses	Net Profit/Loss

Growth Tracker

What helped me stay disciplined this month?

Where did I break my rules?

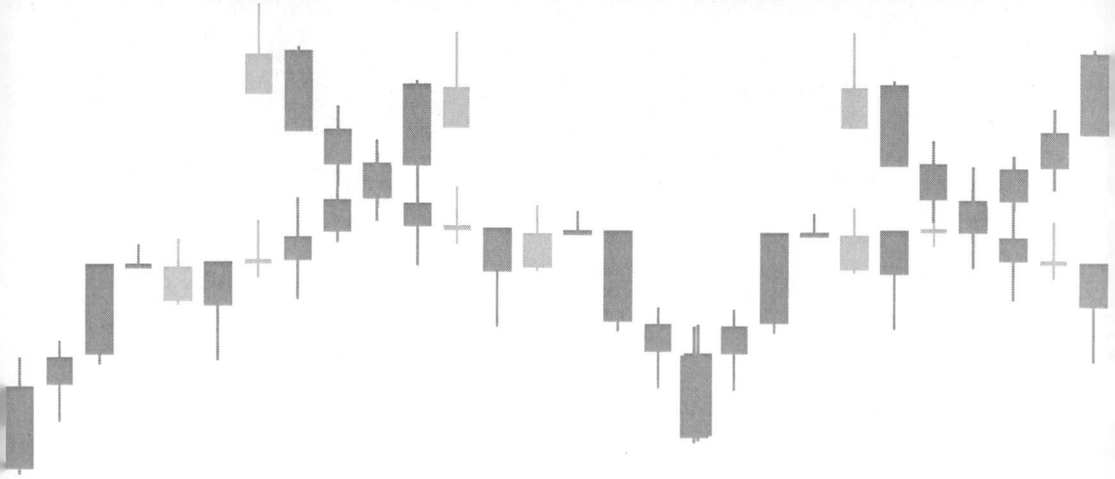

Notes

PROFIT & LOSS MONTHLY SUMMARY

Date	Income	Expenses	Net Profit/Loss

Growth Tracker

What helped me stay disciplined this month?

Where did I break my rules?

PROFIT & LOSS MONTHLY SUMMARY

Date	Income	Expenses	Net Profit/Loss

Growth Tracker

What helped me stay disciplined this month?

Where did I break my rules?

PROFIT & LOSS MONTHLY SUMMARY

Date	Income	Expenses	Net Profit/Loss

Growth Tracker

What helped me stay disciplined this month?

Where did I break my rules?

PROFIT & LOSS MONTHLY SUMMARY

Date	Income	Expenses	Net Profit/Loss

Growth Tracker

What helped me stay disciplined this month?

Where did I break my rules?

PROFIT & LOSS MONTHLY SUMMARY

Date	Income	Expenses	Net Profit/Loss

Growth Tracker

What helped me stay disciplined this month?

Where did I break my rules?

PROFIT & LOSS MONTHLY SUMMARY

Date	Income	Expenses	Net Profit/Loss

Growth Tracker

What helped me stay disciplined this month?

Where did I break my rules?

PROFIT & LOSS MONTHLY SUMMARY

Date	Income	Expenses	Net Profit/Loss

Growth Tracker

What helped me stay disciplined this month?

Where did I break my rules?

FINAL REFLECTION & GROWTH PLAN

The #1 Lesson this Logbook taught me:

____

____

How I'll Apply This in My Future Trading:

____

____

____

"Consistency creates success in futures."

FINAL REFLECTION & GROWTH PLAN

The #2 Lesson this Logbook taught me:

____

____

How I'll Apply This in My Future Trading:

____

____

____

"Consistency creates success in futures."

FINAL REFLECTION & GROWTH PLAN

The #3 Lesson this Logbook taught me:

____

____

How I'll Apply This in My Future Trading:

____

____

____

"Consistency creates success in futures."

FINAL REFLECTION & GROWTH PLAN

The #4 Lesson this Logbook taught me:

____

____

How I'll Apply This in My Future Trading:

____

____

____

"Consistency creates success in futures."

FINAL REFLECTION & GROWTH PLAN

The #5 Lesson this Logbook taught me:

____

____

How I'll Apply This in My Future Trading:

____

____

____

"Consistency creates success in futures."

Final Thoughts!

CONGRATULATIONS!

Thank you for using this logbook!

Explore other publications at www.bengalgeek.com

Scan me!

CERTIFICATE OF ACHIEVEMENT

TRADING MASTERY JOURNEY COMPLETED

This certifies that

____

has successfully completed their trading logbook journey with discipline and growth.

Date: ____________